NATIONAL ANTHEMS
OF THE WORLD

NATIONAL ANTHEMS OF THE WORLD

NINTH EDITION

Edited by
W. L. Reed and M. J. Bristow

CASSELL

Cassell Publishers Limited
Wellington House
125 Strand
London WC2R 0BB

First Published in the U.K. 1960
Second Edition 1963
Third Edition 1969
Fourth Edition 1975
Fifth Edition 1978
Sixth Edition 1985
Seventh Edition 1987
Eighth Edition 1993
Ninth Edition 1997

Distributed in the United States by
Sterling Publishing Co., Inc.,
387 Park Avenue South, New York, N.Y. 10016-8810

British Library Cataloguing-in-Publication Data
A catalogue record for this book is available from the British Library
ISBN 0-304-34925-9

Music and text set by Lancaster Music Setting, Huddersfield
Printed in Great Britain by Bath Press, Bath

$89.95

CONTENTS

PREFACE

There have been several changes and additions of National Anthems since the Eighth Edition of this book was published in 1993.

The following nations have gained independence - Belarus, Bosnia Herzegovina, Eritrea, Kazakhstan, Kyrgyzstan, Macedonia, Marshall Islands, Micronesia, Palau, Tajikistan, Turkmenistan and Uzbekistan. The following nations have adopted new National Anthems - Iran, Moldova, Seychelles and Zimbabwe, whereas Cambodia and Togo have reverted to their original National Anthems. Oman has added words to its National Anthem. The new Anthem of Gibraltar has been included for its particular interest, although the country has not yet achieved independence from the United Kingdom. The European Anthem has been added at the end of the book.

There are examples of some National Anthems where, regrettably, it has not been possible to fit the words to the music, as no vocal scores have been supplied to the editors.

The list of National Days has been revised and updated.

Where a National Anthem is in a language that is not written in the Roman script, the words are given in a transliterated phonetic version.

The editors would like to express their thanks for the valuable help and advice given to them by Dr. T. M. Cartledge, who died in 1993; to the faculty of the School of Oriental and African Studies; to the School of Slavonic and East European Studies at London University; to the BBC World Service; to Reinhard Popp in Germany; to Trevor Adair in Northern Ireland; to Fabio Lazzati in Italy; to George Csüllög of Hungary; to the publishers Philipp Reclam Jun. in Stuttgart and to the various Embassies and High Commissions, who have supplied valuable information concerning their National Anthems.

Effort has been made to trace copyright ownership, and it is regretted if any acknowledgments have been unwittingly omitted. In most cases the version of the melody and the accompaniment is that officially authorised by the State. Where piano arrangements and translations have been specially made, these may not be reproduced without the permission of Cassell.

It is hoped that this Ninth Edition will be a useful reference book, not only for the number of occasions on which it is required to sing or play a particular National Anthem, but also as a record of the aspirations of the whole family of nations.

W.L.R.
M.J.B.
January 1997

AFGHANISTAN

Words by
SULEIMAN LAEQ (*b.* 1930)

Music by
USTAD SALIM SARMAD (*b.* 1928)
Arr. by W. L. REED

1. Ga - ram shah lā ga - ram shah Ta e mu - qua - das la - ma - ra E da - ā - zā - dī la - ma - ra

Adopted in 1978. It has been replaced by a new National Anthem, but details are as yet unobtainable.

2. *Dā inqilābī vatan*
   Os da-kārgarāno de
   Dagha da-zmaro mīrās
   Os da-bāzgarāno de
   Ter-so da-sitam daur
   Vār da-mazdūrāno de
   Muzh pa-nārīvālo-ke
   Sola au urūrī ğvārū
   Muzhan ziyār istunko-ta
   Parākha āzādī ğvārū
   Muzh varta dode ğvārū
   Kor ğvārū kālī ğvārū.

Translation

1. Become hot, become more hot,
   You, the holy sun.
   O sun of freedom,
   O sun of good fortune.
   We through the storm
   Have come to the end of the road.
   We have also traversed the paths of darkness,
   Also the way of light.
   The red road of victory,
   The pure path of brotherhood.

2. Our revolutionary homeland
   Is now in the hands of the workers.
   The inheritance of lions
   Now belongs to the peasants.
   The age of tyranny has passed,
   The turn of the labourers has come.
   We want peace and brotherhood
   Between the peoples of the world.
   We demand more freedom
   For all who toil.
   We want bread for them,
   We want houses and clothes.

ALBANIA

Words by
ALEKSANDER STAVRE DRENOVA (1872 - 1947)

Music by
CIPRIAN PORUMBESCU (1853 - 1883)
Arr. by HENRY COLEMAN

Rreth flam - ur - it të për - ba - shku - ar Me një dë-
shir', me një që - llim, Të gjith' at - je duke‿u be-
tu - ar Të lid - him be - sën për shpë - tim! Prej

Music composed in 1880. Adopted in 1912.

Translation

The flag which in battle unites us
Found us all ready for the oath,
One mind, one aim, until our land
Becomes free from the enemy.

CHORUS

We stand in the battle for right and freedom,
The enemies of the people stand alone,
The hero dedicates his life to our land,
Even in dying he will be brave.

13

ALGERIA

Words by
MUFDI ZAKARIAH (1930-1978)

Music by
MOHAMED FAWZI (1918-1966)
Arr. by TAREK HASSAN

Adopted in 1963.

15

2. *Nah-no Gon-don Fi Sa-bi-l Il hakki Thor-na*
   Wa I-la Iss-tiq-la-li-na Bil-har-bi Kum-na.
   Lam Ya-kon Yoss-gha La-na Lam-ma Na-tak-na
   Fat-ta-khath-na Ran-na-t ͜ Al-ba-roo-di Waz-na.
   Wa Azaf-na Na-gha-ma-t ͜ Al-rash-sha-shi Lah-na
   Wa A-qad-na ͜ Al-azma An Tah-ya ͜ Al-ga-za-ir.
   Fash-ha-doo! Fash-ha-doo! Fash-ha-doo!

3. *Nah-no min Ab-ta-li-na Nad-fa-oo Gon-dan*
   Wa A-la Ash-la-ina Nass-na-oo Mag-dan.
   Wa A-la Ar-wa-he-na Nass-a-do Khul-dan
   Wa A-la Ha-ma-ti-na Nar-fa-o Ban-dan.
   Gab-ha-to ͗ L-tah-ree-ri Aa-tay-na-ki Ah-dan
   Wa A-qad-na ͜ Al-azma An Tah-ya ͜ Al-ga-za-ir.
   Fash-ha-doo! Fash-ha-doo! Fash-ha-doo!

4. *Sar-kha-to ͗ `l-aw-ta-ni min Sa-h Il-fi-da*
   Iss-ma-oo-ha Wass-ta-gee-bo Lin-ni-da
   Wak-to-boo-ha Bi-di-maa Il-sho-ha-daa
   Wak-ra-oo-ha Li-ba-ny ͜ Il-geeli gha-dan.
   Kad Ma-dad-na La-ka Ya Mag-do Ya-da
   Wa A-qad-na Al-azma An Tah-ya ͜ Al-ga-za-ir.
   Fash-ha-doo! Fash-ha-doo! Fash-ha-doo!

French Translation

1. *Par les foudres qui anéantissent,*
   Par les flots de sang pur et sans tache,
   Par les drapeaux flottants qui flottent
   Sur les hauts djebels orgueilleux et fiers,
   Nous jurons nous être révoltés pour vivre ou pour mourir,
   Et nous avons juré de mourir pour que vive l'Algérie!
   Témoignez! Témoignez! Témoignez!

2. *Nous sommes des soldats pour la justice, révoltés,*
   Et pour notre indépendance nous avons engagé le combat,
   Nous n'avons obéi à nulle injonction en nous soulevant.
   Le bruit de la poudre a été notre mesure
   Et le crépitement des mitrailleuses notre chant favori.
   Et nous avons juré de mourir pour que vive l'Algérie!
   Témoignez! Témoignez! Témoignez!

3. *Sur nos héros nous bâtirons une gloire*
   Et sur nos corps nous monterons à l'immortalité,
   Sur nos âmes, nous construirons une armée
   Et de notre espoir nous lèverons l'étendard.
   Front de la libération, nous t'avons prêté serment
   Et nous avons juré de mourir pour que vive l'Algérie!
   Témoignez! Témoignez! Témoignez!

4. *Le cri de la patrie monte des champs de bataille.*
   Ecoutez-le et répondez à l'appel.
   Ecrivez-le dans le sang des martyrs
   Et dictez-le aux générations futures.
   Nous t'avons donné la main, ô gloire,
   Et nous avons juré de mourir pour que vive l'Algérie!
   Témoignez! Témoignez! Témoignez!

1. We swear by the lightning that destroys,
    By the streams of generous blood being shed,
    By the bright flags that wave,
    Flying proudly on the high djebels,
    That we are in revolt, whether to live or to die,
    We are determined that Algeria should live,
    So be our witness- be our witness- be our witness!

2. We are soldiers in revolt for truth
    And we have fought for our independence.
    When we spoke, nobody listened to us,
    So we have taken the noise of gunpowder as our rhythm
    And the sound of machine-guns as our melody,
    We are determined that Algeria should live,
    So be our witness-be our witness- be our witness!

3. From our heroes we shall make an army come to being,
    From our dead we shall build up a glory,
    Our spirits shall ascend to immortality
    And on our shoulders we shall raise the Standard.
    To the nation's Liberation Front we have sworn an oath,
    We are determined that Algeria should live,
    So be our witness- be our witness- be our witness!

4. The cry of the Fatherland sounds from the battlefields.
    Listen to it and answer the call!
    Let it be written with the blood of martyrs
    And be read to future generations.
    Oh, Glory, we have held out our hand to you,
    We are determined that Algeria should live,
    So be our witness-be our witness-be our witness!

ANDORRA

Words by
JOAN BENLLOCH I VIVÓ (1864-1926)

Music by
ENRIC MARFANY BONS (1871-1942)

El gran Car - le - many, mon Pa - re, dels a - larbs em des - lliu - rà,_____ I del cel vi - da em do - nà_____ de Me - rit - xell, la gran Ma - re, Prin - ce - sa nasquí i Pu -

Became officially the National Anthem on 8 September, 1914, the anniversary day of the Jungfrau von Meritxell, patron saint of Andorra.

bi - lla en - tre dues na - cions neu - tral_____ Sols

11

res - to l'ú - ni - ca fi - lla de l'im - pe - ri Car - le -

14

many. Cre - ient i lliu - re on - ze se - gles, cre -

17

ient i lliu - re vull ser. ¡Si - guin els furs mos tu-

20

19

Translation

The great Charlemagne, my Father, liberated me from the Saracens,
And from heaven he gave me life of Meritxell the great Mother.
I was born a Princess, a Maiden neutral between two nations;
I am the only remaining daughter of the Carolingian empire.
Believing and free for eleven centuries, believing and free I will be.
The laws of the land be my tutors, and Princes my defender !
And Princes my defender!

ANGOLA

Words by
MANUEL RUI ALVES MONTEIRO (b. 1941)

Music by
RUI ALBERTO VIEIRA DIAS MINGAO (b. 1939)
Arr. by W. L. REED

1. O Pá - tria, nun - ca mais es - que - ce - re - mos os he-

ró - is do qua - tro de Fe - ve - rei - o. O

Pá - tria, nós sau - da - mos os teus fi - lhos tom-

Adopted in 1975.

ba - dos pe - la nos - sa In - de - pen - dên - cia. Hon -

ra - mos o pas - sa - do e a nos - sa His - tó - ria, con - stru -

in - do no Tra - bal - ho o Ho - mem no - vo, Hon -

ra - mos o pas - sa - do e a nos - sa His - tó - ria, con - stru -

cresc.

cresc.

ção,   pe - lo Po - der Po - pu - lar!   Pá - tria U -

ni - da, Li - ber - da - de, um só Po - vo u - ma só Na - ção!

Translation

2. *Levantemos nossas vozes libertadas*
Para glória dos povos africanos.
Marchemos, combatentes angolanos,
Solidários com os povos oprimidos.
Orgulhosos lutaremos pela Paz
Com as forças progressistas do mundo.
Orgulhosos lutaremos pela Paz
Com as forças progressistas do mundo.

    CHORUS
    Angola, avante!
    Revolução, pelo Poder Popular! } (twice)
    Pátria Unida, Liberdade,
    Um só Povo, uma só Nação!

1. O Fatherland, we shall never forget
The heroes of the Fourth of February.
O Fatherland, we salute your sons
Who died for our independence.
We honour the past and our history
As by our work we build the New Man.

CHORUS
Forward, Angola!
Revolution through the power of the People! } (twice)
A United Country, Freedom,
One People, one Nation!

2. Let us raise our liberated voices
To the glory of the peoples of Africa.
We shall march, Angolan fighters,
In solidarity with oppressed peoples.
We shall fight proudly for Peace
Along with the progressive forces of the world.

CHORUS

25

ANTIGUA AND BARBUDA

Words by
NOVELLE HAMILTON RICHARDS (1917 - 1986)

Music by
WALTER GARNET PICART CHAMBERS (*b.* 1908)
Arr. by W. L. REED

1. Fair Antigua, we salute thee! Proudly we this anthem raise To thy glory and thy beauty. Joyfully we sing the praise Of the virtues,

Originally adopted in 1967 on achieving statehood, and again in 1981 when achieving independence.

all be-stow-èd On thy sons and daugh-ters free;

Ev-er striv-ing, ev-er seek-ing, Dwell in love and un-i-ty.

2. Raise the standard! Raise it boldly!
   Answer now to duty's call
   To the service of thy country,
   Sparing nothing, giving all;
   Gird your loins and join the battle
   'Gainst fear, hate and poverty,
   Each endeavouring, all achieving,
   Live in peace where man is free.

3. God of nations, let Thy blessings
   Fall upon this land of ours;
   Rain and sunshine ever sending,
   Fill her fields with crops and flowers;
   We her children do implore Thee,
   Give us strength, faith, loyalty,
   Never failing, all enduring
   To defend her liberty.

ARGENTINA

Words by
VICENTE LÓPEZ Y PLANES (1785 - 1856)

Music by
BLAS PARERA (1765 - c. 1830)
Arr. by JUAN PEDRO ESNAOLA
and LUIS N. LARETA

Officially adopted on 11 May, 1813, by the General Constituent Assembly. There are nine verses.

tad, li - ber - tad, li - ber - tad! O - id el

ruí - do de ro - tas ca - de - nas; Ved en

tro - no a la no - ble I - gual - dad.

¡Ya— su tro - no dig - ni - si - mo a - brie - ron Las Pro-

30

li - bres del mun - do res - pon - den: ¡Al gran

pue - blo Ar - gen - ti - no, Sa - lud! Y___ los

li - bres del mun - do res - pon - den: ¡Al gran

pue - blo Ar - gen - ti - no, Sa - lud!

Allegro vivace (♩ = 126)

CHORUS

Sean e - ter - nos los lau-

re - les, Que su - pi - mos con - se - guir: Que su-

(♩ = 76)

33

pi - mos con - se - guir: Co - ro - na - dos de glo - ria vi-

lunga

va - mos O— ju - re - mos con glo - ria mo - rir. O ju-

re - mos con glo - ria mo - rir. O ju-

re - mos con glo - ria mo - rir.

Translation

Mortals! Hear the sacred cry;
Freedom! Freedom! Freedom!
Hear the noise of broken chains.
See noble Equality enthroned.
The United Provinces of the South
Have now displayed their worthy throne.
And the free peoples of the world reply; ⎫
We salute the great people of Argentina ! ⎭ (twice)

CHORUS
May the laurels be eternal
That we knew how to win.
Let us live crowned with glory,
Or swear to die gloriously. (three times)

ARMENIA

Words adapted from a poem by
MIQAYÉL GHAZARI NALBANDYAN (1829 - 1866)

Music by
BARSEGH KANACHYAN (1885 - 1967)
Arr. by W. L. REED

Officially adopted on 1 July, 1991.

2. *Aha yeghbayr qez mi drôsh,*
   Zor im dzerqov gordsetsi.
   Gishernerə yes qoun chegha,
   Artasouqov lvatsi. } (twice)

3. *Nayir nran yereq gouynov,*
   Nvirakan mék nshan,
   T'ogh p'oghp'oghi t'shnamou dém,
   T'ogh misht pandsa Hayastan. } (twice)

4. *Amenayn tegh mahə mi é*
   Mard mi angam pit merni,
   Bayts yerani vor iur azgi
   Azatout'yan kə zohvi. } (twice)

Translation by E. V. Gulbekian

1. Land of our fathers, free, independent,
   Which has endured from age to age.
   Its sons and daughters now proclaim } (twice)
   Armenia, sovereign and free.

2. Brother, take this banner,
   Made with my own hands,
   During sleepless nights, } (twice)
   And bathed in my tears.

3. See, it has three colours;
   A single hallowed symbol.
   May it sparkle before the foe, } (twice)
   May Armenia flourish ever!

4. Death is everywhere the same,
   Man is born just once to die,
   But blest is he who gives his life } (twice)
   To defend his nation's freedom.

37

AUSTRALIA
Advance Australia Fair

Words and music by
PETER DODDS McCORMICK (1834 - 1916)
Arr. by W. L. REED

Adopted officially as the National Anthem on 19 April, 1984. The words were then slightly changed. The National Anthem of Australia is also used on Norfolk Island.

CHORUS

2. Beneath our radiant Southern Cross
   We'll toil with hearts and hands;
   To make this Commonwealth of ours
   Renowned of all the lands;
   For those who've come across the seas
   We've boundless plains to share;
   With courage let us all combine
   To Advance Australia fair.

   CHORUS

AUSTRIA

Words by
PAULA VON PRERADOVIĆ (1887 - 1951)

Music by
JOHANN HOLZER (1753 - 1818)*
Arr. by VIKTOR KELDORFER

1. Land der Ber-ge,— Land am Stro-me, Land der Äc-ker,— Land der Do-me, Land der Häm-mer, zu-kunfts-reich! Hei-mat bist— du gro-sser— Söh-ne,

Officially adopted by the Austrian Cabinet on 25 February, 1947.

*Mozart has been claimed as the composer, but the evidence is more in Holzer's favour, according to Austrian scholarship.

2. *Heiss umfehdet, wild umstritten,*
   Liegst dem Erdteil du inmitten
   Einem starken Herzen gleich.
   Hast seit Frühen Ahnentagen
   Hoher Sendung Last getragen,
   Vielgeprüftes Österreich, Vielgeprüftes Österreich.

3. *Mutig in die neuen Zeiten,*
   Frei und gläubig sieh uns schreiten,
   Arbeitsfroh und hoffnungsreich.
   Einig lass in Brüderchören,
   Vaterland, dir Treue schwören,
   Vielgeliebtes Österreich, Vielgeliebtes Österreich.

Translation

1. Land of mountains, land on the River*,
   Land of fields, land of spires,
   Land of hammers, with a rich future,
   You are the home of great sons,
   A nation blessed by its sense of beauty,
   Highly praised Austria, highly praised Austria.

2. Strongly fought for, fiercely contested,
   You are in the centre of the Continent
   Like a strong heart,
   You have borne since the earliest days
   The burden of a high mission,
   Much tried Austria, much tried Austria.

3. Watch us striding free and believing,
   With courage, into new eras,
   Working cheerfully and full of hope,
   In fraternal chorus let us take in unity
   The oath of allegiance to you, our country,
   Our much beloved Austria, our much beloved Austria.

* the Danube

41

AZERBAIJAN

Words by
AHMED JAVAD (1892 - 1937)

Music by
UZEIR GADJIBECOV (1885 - 1948)
Arr. by W. L. REED

The words and music of the National Anthem were written in 1919. Officially adopted on 27 May, 1992.

mas - uad   ya - sha!__   Ooch - ran - gle bay - ra - gin - le   mas - uad   ya - sha!__

Mean - ler - le   jan   goor - ban   ol - de!   Se - nan   har - ba   may - don   ol - de!

Ho - go - gin - dan   ke - chan   as - gar   Ha - ra   beer   gah - ra - man   ol - de!

San   o - la - san   goo - lo - stan,   Sa - na   har__   on   jan   goor - ban!

43

44

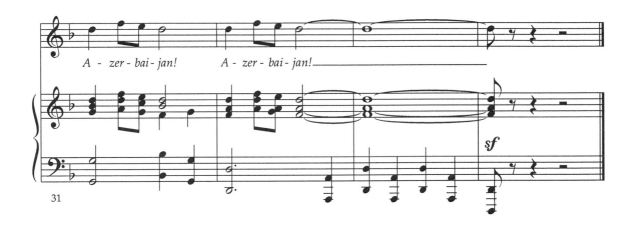

A - zer - bai - jan!   A - zer - bai - jan!

31

Translation

Azerbaijan! Azerbaijan!
O Great Land, your children are heroes.
We are ready to be martyred for you.
We are ready to shed blood for you.
Three-coloured flag, flourish honourably!
Thousands of lives have been sacrificed.
Your bosom has become a battlefield.
Every devoted soldier
Has become a hero.
You are prospering.
My life is always dedicated to you.
My love for you is embedded in my heart
A thousand and one times.
To preserve everything
And to honour her flag
All the youth are willing.
Great Land! Great Land!
Azerbaijan! Azerbaijan!

THE BAHAMAS

Words and music by
TIMOTHY GIBSON (1903 - 1978)
Arr. by W. L. REED

Selected as a result of a competition and adopted when the country became independent on 10 July, 1973.

high. See how the world marks the man - ner of your— bear - ing! Pledge to ex - cel through love and— un - i - ty. Press - ing on - ward, march to - ge - ther to a com - mon loft - ier goal; Stead - y

BAHRAIN

Words by
MOHAMED SUDQI AYYASH (*b.* 1925)

Composer unknown
Arr. by MOHAMED SUDQI AYYASH

Allegretto alla marcia

Bah - rai - no - na____ Ba - la - dol - a -
man____ Wa - ta - nol ki - ram,____ Yah - mi Hi ma - ha A - mi - ru nal Ho -
mam; Qa - mat - a - la - Ha - dy - el - r - e - sa - la - te, Wal A - da - la - ti Wal Sa -

Adopted in 1971.

-lam! A - Shat Daw - la - tol Bah - rain_____ Ba - la - dol - a - rain.

Translation

Our Bahrain,
Country of security,
Nation of hospitality,
Protected by our courageous Amir,
Founded on the principles of the Message,
Justice and Peace,
Long live the State of Bahrain!

BANGLADESH

Words and music by
RABINDRANATH TAGORE (1861 - 1941)*
Arr. by T. M. CARTLEDGE

Allegretto e espressivo, molto legato

Ā-mār so-nār— Bān - glā,— Ā - mi to-māý— bhā - lo - bā - shi,— Ci - rā - din to - mār ā - kās,— to - mār— bā - tas, ā - mār— prā - né—

Officially adopted in April 1971 by the then provisional government; approved by the National Assembly on 13 January, 1972.

* Rabindranath Tagore also wrote the words and music of the National Anthem of India.

2nd time to ⊕

⊕

42

mari hāý,   hāý re O mā,
mari hāý,   hāý re Mā, tor

Fā - gu - ne tor ā - mer ba - ne ghrā - ne pā - gal ka - re,
mu - kher bā - nī ā - mar ka - ne lā - ge, su - dhar ma - to,

48

O mā, a - ghrā - ne tor bha - rā
Mā, tor ba - dan - khā - ni ma - lin

55

kse - te kī de - khe - chi ā - mi kī de -
ha - le, ā - mi na - ýan O mā, ā - mi

61

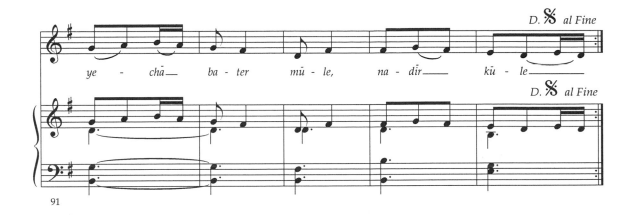

ye - chā — ba - ter mū - le, na - dir —— kū - le ——

91

Translation

My Bengal of gold, I love you.
Forever your skies, your air set my heart in tune
As if it were a flute.
In spring, O mother mine, the fragrance from your mango groves
Makes me wild with joy –
Ah, what a thrill!

In autumn, O mother mine,
In the full-blossomed paddy fields
I have seen spread all over – sweet smiles.
Ah, what a beauty, what shades, what an affection
And what a tenderness!
What a quilt have you spread at the feet of banyan trees
And along the banks of rivers!

O mother mine, words from your lips
Are like nectar to my ears.
Ah, what a thrill!
If sadness, O mother mine, casts a gloom on your face,
My eyes are filled with tears!

BARBADOS

Words by
IRVING LOUIS BURGIE (*b.* 1924)

Music by
VAN ROLAND EDWARDS (1912 - 1985)
Arr. by W. L. REED

1. In— plen-ty and in time of need When this fair land was young. Our— brave fore-fa-thers sowed the seed From which our pride is sprung, A pride that makes no wan-ton boast Of what it has with -

Adopted on 30 November, 1966, upon independence.

his - tory's page With ex - pec - ta - tions great. Strict

guard - ians of our he - ri - tage, Firm crafts - men of our fate.

2. The Lord has been the people's guide
   For past three hundred years.
   With Him still on the people's side
   We have no doubts or fears.
   Upward and onward we shall go,
   Inspired, exulting, free,
   And greater will our nation grow
   In strength and unity.

   CHORUS

BELARUS

Words by
MIKHAS KLIMKOVICH (1899 - 1954)*

Music by
NESTER SAKALOUSKI (1902 - 1950)

Adopted on 24 September, 1955.
* The words are not currently in general use.

BELGIUM

La Brabançonne
(The Song of Brabant)

French words by
CHARLES ROGIER (1800 - 1885)
Flemish words by
R. HERREMAN *

Music by
FRANÇOIS VAN CAMPENHOUT (1779 - 1848)

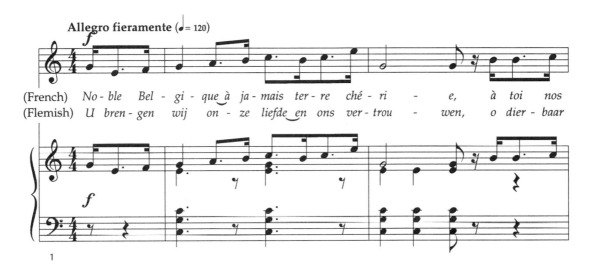

(French) No - ble Bel - gi - que à ja - mais ter - re ché - ri - e, à toi nos
(Flemish) U bren - gen wij on - ze liefde en ons ver - trou - wen, o dier - baar

cœurs,____ à toi nos bras.____ Par le sang pur ré - pan - du pour toi, Pa -
volk,____ o dier - baar land.____ De vaad - ren trouw, zul - len wij de toe - komst

Written and composed during the 1830 revolution. The original French words were by Jenneval, a Belgian officer, but the present version was written in 1860 by Prime Minister Charles Rogier. The Flemish text also underwent several changes.
* Official version of the Flemish words made in 1980. Dates of author unknown.

tri - e. nous le ju - rons d'un seul cri tu vi - vras!_____ Tu vi-
bou - wen, in vreugd' en nood is ons hart U ver - pand._____ Groei en

vras, tou - jours grande et bel - le, et ton in - vin - ci - ble u - ni -
bloei tot heil der ge - slach - ten. wij rei ken el - kaar de brue - der -

té_____ Au - ra pour de - vise im - mor - tel - le, le
hand_____ En wij - den de vro - me ge - dach - ten aan

Translation of the French version by W. L. Reed

Noble Belgium - for ever a dear land -
We give you our hearts and our arms.
By the pure blood spilt for you, our Fatherland,
We swear with one cry - You will live!
You will live, always great and beautiful,
And your invincible unity
Will have as your immortal emblem -
For King, Justice and Liberty!

BELIZE

Words by
SAMUEL ALFRED HAYNES (1898 - 1971)

Music by
SELWYN WALFORD YOUNG (1899 - 1977)
Arr. by W. L. REED

1. O Land of the Free by the Ca - rib Sea, Our man - hood we pledge to thy li - ber - ty! No ty - rants here lin - ger, des - pots must flee This tran - quil ha - ven of de - mo - cra - cy. The

Officially adopted upon independence on 21 September, 1981.

blood of our sires, which hal - lows the sod, Brought

free - dom from slav - 'ry, op - pres - sion's rod, By the

might of truth and the grace of God. No

lon - ger shall__ we be hew - ers of wood. A -

CHORUS

rise,   ye   sons   of   the Bay - men's

clan!   Put   on   your   ar - mour,

clear   the   land!   Drive back   the

ty - rants,   let   des - pots___ flee!

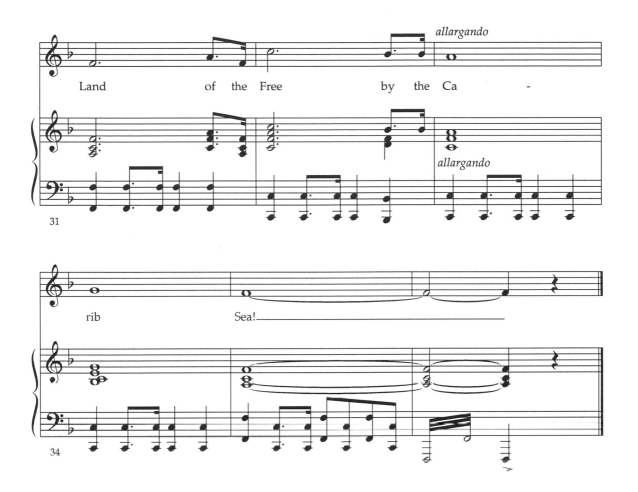

2. Nature has blessed thee with wealth untold,
   O'er mountains and valleys where prairies roll;
   Our fathers, the Baymen, valiant and bold
   Drove back th'invader, this heritage bold
   From proud Rio Hondo to old Sarstoon,
   Through coral isle, over blue lagoon,
   Keep watch with the angels, the stars and moon.
   For freedom comes tomorrow's noon.

   CHORUS

BÉNIN

L'Aube Nouvelle
(The Dawn of a New Day)

Words and music by
GILBERT JEAN DAGNON (*b*. 1926)
Arr. by HENRY COLEMAN

1. Ja - dis à son ap - pel, nos aï - eux sans fai - bles - se Ont su a - vec cou - rage, ar - deur, pleins d'al - lé - gres - se Li -

Adopted as the National Anthem of Dahomey at the declaration of independence on 30 July, 1960.
The chorus is usually sung on its own.

vrer au prix du sang des com - bats é - cla - tants. Ac - cou-

rez vous aus-si, bâ - tis - seurs du pré - sent, Plus forts dans

l'u ni té, chaqu' jour à la tâ - che, Pour la

pos - té - ri - té, cons - trui - sez sans re - lâ - che.

2. *Quand partout souffle un vent de colère et de haine,*
   Béninois, sois fier, et d'une âme sereine,
   Confiant dans l'avenir, regarde ton drapeau!
   Dans le vert tu liras l'espoir du renouveau,
   De tes aïeux le rouge évoque le courage;
   Des plus riches trésors le jaune est le présage.

   CHORUS

70

3. *Tes monts ensoleillés, tes palmiers, ta verdure,*
   Cher Bénin, partout font ta vive parure.
   Ton sol offre à chacun la richesse des fruits.
   Bénin, désormais que tes fils tous unis
   D'un fraternel élan partagent l'espérance
   De te voir à jamais heureux dans l'abondance.

   CHORUS

Translation by Elizabeth P. Coleman

1. Formerly, at her call, our ancestors
   Knew how to engage in mighty battles
   With strength, courage, ardour, and full of joy, but at the price of blood.
   Builders of the present, you too, join forces
   Each day for the task stronger in unity.
   Build without ceasing for posterity.

   CHORUS
   Children of Bénin, arise!
   The resounding cry of freedom
   Is heard at the first light of dawn;
   Children of Bénin, arise!

2. When all around there blows a wind of anger and hate:
   Citizen of Bénin, be proud, and in a calm spirit
   Trusting in the future, behold your flag!
   In the green you read hope of spring;
   The red signifies the courage of your ancestors;
   The yellow foretells the richest treasures.

   CHORUS

3. Beloved Bénin, your sunny mountains, palm trees, and green pastures
   Show everywhere your brightness;
   Your soil offers everyone the richest fruits.
   Bénin, from henceforth your sons are united
   With one brotherly spirit sharing the hope of seeing you
   Enjoy abundance and happiness for ever.

   CHORUS

BHUTAN

Words by
GYALDUN DASHO THINLEY DORJI (1914 - 1966)

Music by
AKU TONGMI (*b*. 1913)
Transcribed and arranged by
W. L. REED

Adopted in 1953.

Druk tsendhen koipi gyelkhap na
Loog ye ki tenpa chongwai gyon
Pel mewang ngadhak rinpo chhe
Ku jurmey tenching chhap tsid pel
Chho sangye ten pa goong dho gyel
Bang dhe kyed nyima shar warr sho.

Translation

In the Thunder Dragon Kingdom
Adorned with sandalwood,
The protector who guards the
Teachings of the dual system,
He, the precious and glorious ruler,
Causes dominion to spread,
While his unchanging person abides
In constancy.
As the doctrine of the Lord Buddha
Flourishes,
May the sun of peace and happiness
Shine on the people!

BOLIVIA

Words by
JOSÉ IGNACIO DE SANJINÉS (1786 - 1864)

Music by
LEOPOLDO BENEDETTO VINCENTI (1815 - 1914)

Played for the first time in 1842 and adopted the same year.

li - bre ya li - bre_es - te sue - lo, Ya__ ce - só su - ser - vil__ con - di-

ción. Al es - truen - do mar - cial que a - yer fue - ra Y al cla-

mor__ de la gue - rra ho - rro - ro - so, Si - guen hoy__ en con - tras - te ar - mo-

nio - so Dul - ces him - nos de paz__ y__ de u - nion. Si - guen

2. *Aqui alzó la justicia su trono,*
   Que la vil opresión desconoca.
   Y este timbre glorioso legóse.
   Libertad! Libertad! Libertad!
   Que los hijos del grande Bolívar
   Han ya mil y mil veces jurado,
   Morir antes que ver humillado
   De la Patria el augusto pendón.

   CHORUS

3. *Loor eterno a los bravos guerreros*
   Cuyo heroico valor y firmeza
   Conquistaron las glorias que empieza.
   Hoy Bolivia feliz a gozar.
   Que sus nombres el mármol y el bronce
   A remotas edades trasmitan
   Y en sonoros cantares repitan
   Nuestros hijos y nietos a par.

   CHORUS

Translation by T. M. Cartledge

1. Bolivians, a favourable destiny
   Has crowned our vows and longings;
   This land is free,
   Your servile state has ended.
   The martial turmoil of yesterday
   And the horrible clamour of war
   Are followed today, in harmonious contrast, } (twice)
   By sweet hymns of peace and unity.

   CHORUS

   We have kept the lofty name of our country
   In glorious splendour,
   And on its altars we once more swear
   To die, rather than live as slaves.   } (three times)

2. This innocent and beautiful land,
   Which owes its name to Bolívar,
   Is the happy homeland where men
   Enjoy the benefits of good fortune and peace.
   For the sons of the great Bolívar
   Have sworn, thousands upon thousands of times,
   To die rather than see the country's   } (twice)
   Majestic flag humiliated.

   CHORUS

3. Eternal praise to the brave warriors
   Whose heroic valour and firmness
   Conquered the glories that now
   A happy Bolivia begins to enjoy!
   Let their names, in marble and in bronze,
   Transmit to remote ages
   And in resounding song repeat the call: } (twice)
   Freedom! Freedom! Freedom!

   CHORUS

BOSNIA HERZEGOVINA

Words and music by
DINO DERVIŠHALIDOVIĆ *
Arr. by RANKO RIHTMAN
and W. L. REED

Adopted on 24 November, 1995.

* Dates not yet available.

Je - dna si_ je - di - na, Bo - sna i Her - ce - go - vi - na.

13

2. *Bog nek te sačuva*
   Za pokoljenja nova.
   Zemljo mojih snova
   Mojih pradjedova.

CHORUS

Translation by Paul Tvrtković

1. To you, O ancient land,
   Running from the sea to the Sava,
   Running from the Drina to the Une,
   I give you my allegiance.

   CHORUS
   You are the only one,
   My homeland, my homeland.
   You are the only one,
   By Bosnia Herzegovina.

2. God save you
   For generations to come,
   The land of my dreams,
   The land of my fathers.

   CHORUS

BOTSWANA

Words and music by
KGALEMANG TUMEDISCO MOTSETE (1900 - 1974)
Arr. by W. L. REED

Officially adopted upon independence on 30 September, 1966.

2. *Ina lentle la tumo*
   La chaba ya Botswana,
   Ka kutlwano le kagisano,
   E bopagantswe mmogo.

CHORUS

Translation

2. Word of beauty and of fame,
   The name Botswana to us came.
   Through our unity and harmony,
   We'll remain at peace as one.

CHORUS

BRAZIL

Words by
JOAQUIM OSÓRIO DUQUE ESTRADA (1870 - 1927)

Music by
FRANCISCO MANOEL DA SILVA (1795 - 1865)

The music was written in 1831 on the accession of Emperor Dom Pedro II.
In 1922 a new text was officially adopted and the same tune retained.

ma - da, I - do - la - tra - da, Sal - ve! Sal - ve! Bra -

sil, um so - nho in - ten - so, um ra - io ví - vi - do De a -

mor e de es - pe - ran - ça à ter - ra des - ce, Se em

teu for - mo - so céu, ri - so - nho e lím - pi - do, A i -

ma - gem do Cru - zei - ro res - plan - de - ce. Gi -

gan - te pe - la pró - pria na - tu - re - za, És

be - lo, és for - te, im - pá - vi - do co - los - so. E o

teu fu - tu - ro es - pe - lha es - sa gran - de - za! ___ Ter - ra a - do -

2. *Deitado eternamente em berço esplêndido,*
   Ao som do mar e à luz do céu profundo,
   Fulguras, ó Brasil, florão da América,
   Iluminado ao sol do novo mundo!
   Do que a terra mais garrida
   Teus risonhos, lindos campos têm mais flores;
   "Nossos bosques têm mais vida,"
   "Nossa vida" no teu seio "mais amores."

   Ó Pátria amada, Idolatrada, Salve! Salve!

   Brasil, de amor eterno seja o símbolo
   O lábaro que ostentas estrelado,
   E diga o verde-louro dessa flâmula:
   "Paz no futuro e glória no passado."
   Mas, se ergues da justiça a clava forte,
   Verás que um filho teu não foge à luta
   Nem teme, quem te adora, a própria morte.

   CHORUS
   Terra adorada, Entre outras mil, Es tu, Brasil,
   Ó Pátria amada! Dos filhos deste solo és mãe gentil,
   Pátria amada, Brasil!

1. There was heard, from Ypiranga's placid banks,
   The resounding cry of a heroic people,
   And the sun of freedom, in bright rays,
   Shone at this moment in the homeland's skies.
   As the promise of this equality
   Was secured by our strong arms,
   In your bosom, O Freedom,
   We are ready to die.

   O beloved, idolized homeland, hail, hail!
   Brazil, a vivid dream, a lively ray
   Of love and hope settles on the earth,
   As in your beautiful sky, smiling and limpid,
   The image of the Southern Cross shines resplendent.
   A giant by nature, you are beautiful,
   Strong, an intrepid colossus,
   And your future mirrors this grandeur.

   CHORUS
   O land we adore, among a thousand others
   You are the beloved one.
   You are the gentle mother of the sons of this land,
   Beloved homeland, Brazil!

2. Eternally laid in a splendid cradle,
   To the sound of the sea and the light from the depths of the sky,
   Brazil, you gleam, fleuron of the Americas,
   Illuminated by the sun of the New World.
   Your smiling, lovely fields have more flowers
   Than the most attractive land elsewhere,
   Our forests have more life,
   Our life in your bosom more love.

   O beloved, idolized homeland, hail, hail!
   Brazil, may you have as eternal symbol
   The starry banner you display,
   And may the green laurel of this pennant speak
   Of peace in the future and glory in the past.
   But if you raise a strong cudgel in the name of justice,
   You will see that a son of yours does not run from a fight,
   Nor does one who adores you fear death.

   CHORUS

BRUNEI DARUSSALAM

Words by
PENGIRAN HAJI MOHAMED YUSUF BIN
PENGIRAN HAJI ABDUL RAHIM (b. 1923)

Music by
AWANG HAJI BESAR BIN SAGAP (1914 - 1988)
Arr. by W. L. REED

Composed in 1947 through the initiative of a group of youths who decided that their country should have a National Anthem, and chose two of their number to write and compose it. It was officially adopted in 1951. The country became independent on 1 January, 1984.

Hi - dup sen - to - sa Ne - ga - ra dan Sul - tan,

I - la - hi se - la - mat - kan Bru - nei Da - rus - sa - lam.

Translation

Oh God, Long live our Majesty the Sultan;
Justice and Sovereignty in sheltering
Our country and leading our people;
Prosperity to our Nation and Sultan.
God save Brunei Darussalam.

BULGARIA

Words and music by
TSVETAN TSVETKOV RADOSLAVOV (1863 - 1931)

Original words and music were composed by Radoslavov while still a student in 1885, and on his way to fight in the Serbo-Bulgarian War. It quickly became popular. It was arranged as the National Anthem, replacing the previous Communist Anthem in 1964.

There is a longer version, but the above is the one that is usually sung.

CHORUS

Mee - la Ro - dee - no, (Ro-dee-no,) Tee see ze - men ra_ yee,—

Tvo_yee - ta hu-bost, tvo_yee - ta pre-lest, Ah, te nya-mat

1. kray_ee!

2. kray_ee!

Translation by Katya Boyadjieva

Proudly rise the Balkan peaks,
At their feet Blue Danube flows;
Over Thrace the sun is shining,
Pirin looms in purple glow.

CHORUS
Oh, dear native land,
Earthly paradise!
For your loveliness, your beauty
E'er will charm our eyes. } (twice)

94

BURKINA FASO

Words by
THOMAS SANKARA (1949 - 1987)

Composer unknown
Arr. by W. L. REED

Adopted on 2 August, 1984.

1. *Contre la férule humiliante il y a déjà mille ans,*
   La rapacité venue de loin les asservir il y a cent ans.
   Contre la cynique malice métamorphosée
   En néocolonialisme et ses petits servants locaux
   Beaucoup flanchèrent et certains résistèrent.
   Mais les échecs, les succès, la sueur, le sang
   Ont fortifié notre peuple courageux et fertilisé sa lutte héroïque.

   CHORUS
   Et une seule nuit a rassemblé en elle
   L'histoire de tout un peuple.
   Et une seule nuit a déclenché sa marche triomphale
   Vers l'horizon du bonheur.
   Une seule nuit a réconcilié notre peuple
   Avec tous les peuples du monde,
   A la conquête de la liberté et du progrès
   La Patrie ou la mort, nous vaincrons.

2. *Nourris à la source vive de la Révolution,*
   Les engagés volontaires de la liberté et de la paix
   Dans l'énergie nocturne et salutaire du 4 août
   N'avaient pas que les armes à la main, mais aussi et surtout
   La flamme au cœur pour légitimement libérer
   Le Faso à jamais des fers de tous ceux qui
   Çà et là en polluaient l'âme sacrée de l'indépendance, de la souveraineté.

   CHORUS

3. *Et séant désormais en sa dignité recouvrée*
   L'amour et l'honneur en partage avec l'humanité,
   Le peuple du Burkina chante un hymne à la victoire,
   A la gloire du travail libérateur, émancipateur.
   A bas l'exploitation de l'homme par l'homme!
   Hé en avant pour le bonheur de tout homme,
   Par tous les hommes aujourd'hui et demain, par tous les hommes ici et pour toujours!

   CHORUS

4. *Révolution populaire notre sève nourricière.*
   Maternité immortelle du progrès à visage d'homme.
   Foyer éternel de démocratie consensuelle,
   Où enfin l'identité nationale a droit de cité,
   Où pour toujours l'injustice perd ses quartiers,
   Et où, des mains des bâtisseurs d'un monde radieux
   Mûrissent partout les moissons de vœux patriotiques, brillent les soleils infinis de joie.

   CHORUS

Translation by K. Jonathan Fryer

1. Against the humiliating bondage of a thousand years
    Rapacity came from afar to subjugate them for a hundred years.
    Against the cynical malice in the shape
    Of neo-colonialism and its petty local servants,
    Many gave in and certain others resisted.
    But the frustrations, the successes, the sweat, the blood
    Have fortified our courageous people and fertilised its heroic struggle.

    CHORUS
    And one single night has drawn together
    The history of an entire people,
    And one single night has launched its triumphal march
    Towards the horizon of good fortune.
    One single night has brought together our people
    With all the peoples of the World,
    In the acquisition of liberty and progress.
    Motherland or death, we shall conquer.

2. Nourished in the lively source of the Revolution,
    The volunteers for liberty and peace
    With their nocturnal and beneficial energies of the 4th of August
    Had not only hand arms, but also and above all
    The flame in their hearts lawfully to free
    Faso forever from the fetters of all those who
    Here and there were polluting the sacred soul of independence and sovereignty.

    CHORUS

3. And seated henceforth in rediscovered dignity,
    Love and honour partnered with humanity,
    The people of Burkina sing a victory hymn
    To the glory of the work of liberation and emancipation.
    Down with exploitation of man by man!
    Forward for the good of every man
    By all men of today and tomorrow, by every man here and always!

    CHORUS

4. Popular revolution our nourishing sap,
    Undying motherhood of progress in the face of man.
    Eternal hearth of agreed democracy,
    Where at last national identity has the right to freedom,
    Where injustice has lost its place forever,
    And where from the hands of builders of a glorious world
    Everywhere harvests of patriotic vows ripen and suns of boundless joy shine.

    CHORUS

BURUNDI

Words by a commission presided over by
JEAN-BAPTISTE NTAHOKAJA (*b.* 1920)

Music prepared by
MARC BARENGAYABO (*b.* 1934)
Arr. by W. L. REED

Bu - rŭ - ndi bwâ - cu, Bu - rŭ - ndi bu - hĭ - re,

Shī - nga i - cŭ - mu mu ma - shī - nga, Ga - ha i - ntă - he y'ŭ - bu - ga - bo

ku bu - gī - ngo. Wa - rá - pfu - nywe ntí - wa - pfû - ye,

Adopted in June 1962.

Wa - rá - ha - bī - shi - jwe ntí - wa - ha - ba - bu - ka,　　U -

Ha - gu - ru- ka- na,u-ha - gu-ru-ka - na, u - Ha-gu-ru-ka- na,u-bu-ga-bo u - rî -

kū - ki-ra.　Ko - me-rwa - ma - shyí - n'á - ma - kú - ngu,

Hā - bwa i-mpŭ-ndu n-â - bâ - we,I - sā - mí-ra-ne mu ma-shī-nga̬i-sā - mí-

French Translation by Jean-Baptiste Ntahokaja

Cher Burundi, ô doux pays,
Prends place dans le concert des nations.
En tout bien, tout honneur, accédé à l'indépendance,
Mutilé et meurtri, tu es demeuré maître de toi-même.

L'heure venue, tu t'es levé
Et fièrement tu t'es hissé au rang des peuples libres.
Reçois donc le compliment des nations,
Agrée l'hommage de tes enfants.
Qu'à travers l'univers retentisse ton nom.

Cher Burundi, héritage sacré de nos aïeux,
Reconnu digne de te gouverner,
Au courage tu allies le sentiment de l'honneur.
Chante la gloire de ta liberté reconquise.

Cher Burundi, digne objet de notre plus tendre amour,
A ton noble service nous vouons nos bras, nos cœurs et nos vies.
Veuille Dieu, qui nous a fait don de toi, te conserver à notre vénération,
Sous l'égide de l'Unité,
Dans la paix, la joie et la prospérité.

Translation (of French Version) by T. M. Cartledge

Beloved Burundi, gentle country,
Take your place in the concert of nations,
Acceding to independence with honourable intentions.
Wounded and bruised, you have remained master of yourself.

When the hour came, you arose,
Lifting yourself proudly into the ranks of free peoples.
Receive, then, the congratulations of the nations
And the homage of your sons.
May your name ring out through the universe.

Beloved Burundi, sacred heritage from our forefathers,
Recognised as worthy of self-government,
With your courage you also have a sense of honour.
Sing the glory of liberty conquered again.

Beloved Burundi, worthy of our tenderest love,
We vow to your noble service our hands and hearts and lives.
May God, who gave you to us, keep you for us to venerate,
Under the shield of unity,
In peace, joy and prosperity.

CAMBODIA
Nokoreach

Words by
CHUON NAT (1883 - 1969)

Adapted from a Cambodian folk song
Arr. by W. L. REED

1. Som pouk tep - da rak sa moha khsath yeung———— oy ben roung roeung doy chey mon - kol—— srey sour - sdey Yeung Khnom preah ang som chrok Krom moloup preah Ba - ro -

Originally adopted in 1941, reaffirmed in 1947, replaced in 1976 and restored on 21 September, 1993.

mey———————— Ney preah No - rop - dey vong Khsat - tra del sang preah sat

thmâr Kroup Kraung dèn Khmer bo - rann thkoeung thkann.

2. *Prasath séla kombang kan dal prey*
   Kuor oy srâmay noeuk dâl yuos sak Moha Nokor
   Cheat Khmer dauch Thmar kong vong nây lâar rung peung chom hor.
   Yeung sang Khim por pheap preng samnang robuos Kampuchea.
   Moha râth koeut mieñ you ang veanh hey.

3. *Kroup vath aram lû tè so sap thoeur*
   Sot doy am nô rom lik koun poth sasna
   Chol yeung chea neak thioeur thiak smos smak tam bêp donnta
   Kong tè thévoda nùng chuoy chrom chrèng phkôt phkang pra yoch oy
   Dol prateah Khmer chea Moha Nokor.

French Translation

1. *Que le ciel protège notre Roi*
   Et lui dispense le bonheur et la gloire.
   Qu'il règne sur nos cœurs et sur nos destinées,
   Celui qui, héritier des Souverains bâtisseurs,
   Gouverne le fier et vieux Royaume.

2. *Les temples dorment dans la forêt,*
   Rappelant la grandeur du Moha Nokor.
   Comme le roc, la race khmère est éternelle,
   Ayons confiance dans le sort du Campuchéa,
   L'Empire qui défie les années.

3. *Les chants montent dans le pagodes*
   A la gloire de la Sainte foi Bouddhique.
   Soyons fidèles aux croyances de nos pères.
   Ainsi le ciel prodiguera-t-il tous ses bienfaits
   Au vieux pays khmer, le Moha Nokor.

English Translation

1. Heaven protects our King
   And gives him happiness and glory
   To reign over our souls and our destinies,
   The one being, heir of the Sovereign builders,
   Guiding the proud old Kingdom.

2. Temples are asleep in the forest,
   Remembering the splendour of Moha Nokor.
   Like a rock the Khmer race is eternal.
   Let us trust in the fate of Campuchea,
   The empire which challenges the ages.

3. Songs rise up from the pagodas
   To the glory of holy buddhistic faith.
   Let us be faithful to our ancestors' belief.
   Thus heaven will lavish its bounty
   Towards the ancient Khmer country, the Moha Nokor.

CAMEROON
Chant de Ralliement

Words by
RENÉ DJAM AFAME (1910 - 1981)
English versification by
T. M. CARTLEDGE

Music by
RENÉ DJAM AFAME (1910 - 1981)
SAMUEL MINKIO BAMBA (*b.* 1911)
and MOÏSE NYATTE NKO'O (1910 - 1978)
Arr. by HENRY COLEMAN

1. O Ca - me - roun, ber - ceau de nos an - cê - tres, Va, de - bout, et ja - loux de ta li - ber - té. Comme un so - leil, ton dra - peau fier doit ê - tre Un sym -

1. O Ca - me - roon, thou cra - dle of our fa - thers, Proud - ly ral - ly to de - fend your lib - er - ty. And like the sun, your flag will be re - splend - ent, As a

Adopted as the unofficial National Anthem in 1948, it became the official National Anthem on 10 May, 1957. The words were substantially changed in 1978.

bole ar-dent de foi et d'u-ni-té._____ Que_____
sym-bol of your faith and u-ni-ty._____ May_____

tous tes en-fants du____ Nord au Sud, De_____
all your chil-dren fol-low the com-mand, From_____

l'Est à l'Ou-est soient tout a-mour!_____ Te ser-vir
East and____ West to give their heart,_____ Their on-ly

que ce soit____ leur____ seul____ but Pour_____
wish____ to____ serve____ their____ land And__ with

CHORUS

rem - plir leur de - voir tou - jours.
con - stan - cy play their part.

Chère Pa - tri - e, terre ché - ri - e, Tu
This our land that we all love so, On

es no - tre seul et vrai bon - heur. No - tre
you our whole hap - pi - ness is stayed. You're our

joie et no - tre vi - e, A toi l'a -
joy and you're our life too; To you be

mour et le grand hon - neur.
hon - our and love dis - played.

2. *Tu es la tombe où dorment nos pères,*
   Le jardin que nos aïeux ont cultivé.
   Nous travaillons pour te rendre prospère,
   Un beau jour enfin nous serons arrivés.
   De l'Afrique sois fidèle enfant
   Et progresse toujours en paix,
   Espérant que tes jeunes enfants
   T'aimeront sans bornes à jamais.

   CHORUS

2. You are the tomb where our fathers are resting,
   You're the garden they prepared and they conceived,
   We work that you may become fair and prosp'rous,
   And one day at last we'll see it all achieved.
   May you be a faithful child of Africa,
   Advancing steadily in peace,
   In hope that ev'ry young child of yours
   Will love you untiI time shall cease.

   CHORUS

CANADA

Words by
SIR ADOLPHE BASILE ROUTHIER (1839 - 1920)
English version by
ROBERT STANLEY WEIR (1856 - 1926)

Music by
CALIXA LAVALLÉE (1842 - 1891)
Arr. by W. L. REED

Officially adopted on 1 July, 1980.

Croix! Ton his-toire est une é - po-pé - e Des
free! From___ far and wide, O___ Ca - na-da! We

CHORUS

plus bril-lants___ ex - ploits. Et ta va-leur,
stand on guard___ for___ thee. God keep our land

de foi trem-pé - e, Pro - té - ge -
glo - rious and free!_____ O Ca - na -

ra nos foy - ers et nos droits,
da! we stand on guard for thee,

Pro - té - ge - ra nos foy - ers et nos droits.
O Ca - na - da! we stand on guard for thee.

2. *Sous l'œil de Dieu, près du fleuve géant,*
   Le Canadien grandit en espérant.
   Il est né d'une race fière,
   Béni fut son berceau,
   Le ciel a marqué sa carriére,
   Dans ce monde nouveau.

CHORUS

2. O Canada! Where pines and maples grow,
   Great prairies spread and lordly rivers flow,
   How dear to us thy broad domain,
   From East to Western sea!
   Thou land of hope for all who toil!
   Thou True North strong and free!

CHORUS

CAPE VERDE

Words and music by
AMILCAR LOPES CABRAL (1924 -1973)

Allegro moderato, alla marcia

1. Sol, su - or e o ver - de e mar,

Sé - cu - los de dor e es - peran - ça: Es - ta é a ter - ra dos

Officially adopted on 5 July, 1975. This National Anthem is the same as that of Guinea-Bissau.

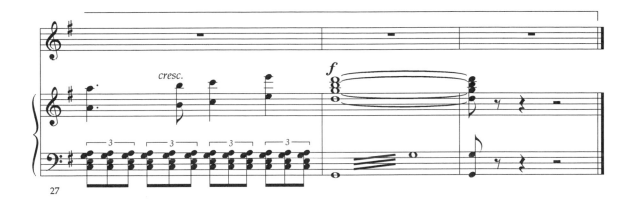

27

2. *Ramos do mesmo tronco,*
   Olhos na mesma luz:
   Esta é a força da nossa união!
   Cantem o mar e a terra
   A madrugada eo sol
   Que a nossa luta fecundou.

   CHORUS

Translation

1. Sun, sweat, verdure and sea,
   Centuries of pain and hope;
   This is the land of our ancestors.
   Fruit of our hands,
   Of the flower of our blood:
   This is our beloved country.

   CHORUS
   Long live our glorious country!
   The banner of our struggle
   Has fluttered in the skies.
   Forward, against the foreign yoke!
   We are going to build
   Peace and progress   }
   In our immortal country!   } (twice)

2. Branches of the same trunk,
   Eyes in the same light;
   This is the force of our unity!
   The sea and the land,
   The dawn and the sun are singing
   That our struggle has borne fruit!

   CHORUS

117

CENTRAL AFRICAN REPUBLIC
La Renaissance

Words by
BARTHÉLÉMY BOGANDA (1910 - 1959)*

Music by
HERBERT PEPPER (*b*. 1912)†

O Cen - tra - fri - que, ô ber - ceau des Ban - tous! Re - prends ton droit au res - pect, à la vie! Long - temps sou - mis, long - temps bri - mé par tous, Mais de ce jour bri -

Adopted by the National Assembly on 25 May, 1960.

* The words are by the first President of the Central African Republic.

† Herbert Pepper also wrote the music of the National Anthem of Sénégal.

santla ty - ran - nie. Dans le tra - vail, l'ordre et la di - gni - té,

Tu re - con - quiers ton droit, ton u - ni - té, Et pour fran - chir cette

é - ta - pe nou - vel - le, De nos an - cê - tres la voix— nous ap - pel - le.

CHORUS

Au tra - vail dans l'ordre et la di - gni - té, Dans le res - pect du

droit dans l'u - ni - té, Bri - sant la mi - sè - re et la ty - ran - nie,

Bran - diss - ant l'é - ten - dard_____ de la Pa - trie._____

Translation by T. M. Cartledge

Oh! Central Africa, cradle of the Bantu!
Take up again your right to respect, to life!
Long subjugated, long scorned by all,
But, from today, breaking tyranny's hold.
Through work, order and dignity
You reconquer your rights, your unity,
And to take this new step
The voice of our ancestors calls us.

CHORUS
To work! In order and dignity,
In the respect for rights and in unity,
Breaking poverty and tyranny,
Holding high the flag of the Fatherland.

CHAD

Words by
LOUIS GIDROL (*b.* 1922)
and students of St. Paul's School

Music by
PAUL VILLARD (1899 -1986)
Arr. by Col. P. DUPONT

Peu - ple Tcha - dien, de - bout et à l'ou - vra - ge! Tu as con-
quis ta terre et ton droit; Ta li - ber - té naî-

Composed for the proclamation of independence in January, 1960.

yeux, pa - ci - fique, a - vance en chan - tant, Fi - dèle à tes an -

ciens qui te re - gar - dent.

D. %al Fine

Translation by T. M. Cartledge

CHORUS
People of Chad, arise and take up the task!
You have conquered the soil and won your rights;
Your freedom will be born of your courage.
Lift up your eyes, the future is yours.

VERSE
Oh, my Country, may God protect you,
May your neighbours admire your children.
Joyful, peaceful, advance as you sing,
Faithful to your fathers who are watching you.

CHORUS

CHILE

Words by
EUSEBIO LILLO ROBLES (1826 - 1910)
and BERNARDO DE VERA Y PINTADO (1789 - 1826)

Music by
RAMÓN CARNICER Y BATTLE (1780 - 1855)

The music was adopted on 17 September, 1847, the words on 12 August, 1909 and it was recognised officially on 27 June, 1941. There are six verses.

co - pia fe - liz____ del E - dén.   Ma - jes -

tuo - sa es la blan - ca mon - ta - ña   Que te

dió por ba - luar - te el Se - ñor,   Que te

dió por ba - luar - te el Se - ñor,   Y e - se

mar——— que tran - qui - lo te ba - ña Te pro -

me - te fu - tu - ro es - plen - dor,——— Y——— e - se

mar——— que tran - qui - lo te ba - ña Te——— pro -

me - te——— fu - tu - ro es - plen - dor.

cresc.

CHORUS

Dul - - - - ce Pa - tria, re - ci - be - los - vo - tos Con que Chi - le en tus a - ras - ju - ró, Que o la

tum - ba se - rás de los li - bres O el a-

si - lo con - tra la o - pre - sión, Que o la

tum - ba se rás de los li - bres O el a-

si - lo con - tra la o - pre - sión, Que o la tum - ba se - rás de los

li - bres   O el   a - si - lo con - tra la o - pre-

51

sión,   O el   a - si - lo con - tra la o pre-

53

sión,   O el   a - si - lo con - tra la o - pre-

55

sión.

ff

57

130

2. *Vuestros nombres, valientes soldados*
   Que habéis sido de Chile el sostén,
   Nuestros pechos los llevan grabados;
   Lo sabrán nuestros hijos también.
   Sean ellos el grito de muerte
   Que lancemos marchando a lidiar,   } (twice)
   Y, sonando en la boca del fuerte,
   Hagan siempre al tirano temblar.   } (twice)

   CHORUS

                    Translation by T. M. Cartledge

1. Chile, your sky is a pure blue,
   Pure breezes blow across you,
   And your field, embroidered with flowers,
   Is a happy copy of Eden.
   Majestic is the snow-covered mountain
   That was given to you by the Lord as a bastion, } (twice)
   And the sea that tranquilly washes your shore
   Promises future splendour for you.   } (twice)

   CHORUS
   Gentle homeland, accept the vows
   Given, Chile, on your altars,
   That you be either the tomb of the free   } (three times)
   Or a refuge from oppression.   } (twice)

2. Your names, gallant soldiers
   Who have been Chile's support,
   Will be carried engraved on our hearts;
   Our sons shall know this too.
   May they be the battle cry
   Uttered as we march into combat,   } (twice)
   And, resounding in the mouth of the strong,
   May they ever make the tyrant tremble.   } (twice)

   CHORUS

131

CHINA
March of the Volunteers

Words by
TIAN HAN (1898 - 1968)

Music by
NIE ER (1912 - 1935)

This song was written in 1935. On 27 September, 1949 it was officially approved as the National Anthem. New words were adopted on 5 March, 1978, but in 1982 the original words were restored.

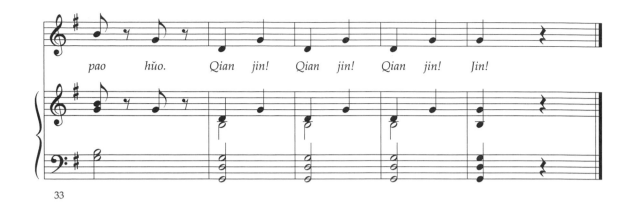

pao   hǔo.   Qian   jin!   Qian   jin!   Qian   jin!   Jin!

33

Translation

Arise, ye who refuse to be slaves!
With our flesh and blood, let us build our new Great Wall!
The Chinese nation faces its greatest danger.
From each one the urgent call for action comes forth.
Arise! Arise! Arise!
Millions with but one heart,
Braving the enemy's fire.
March on!
Braving the enemy's fire.
March on ! March on! March on! On!

COLOMBIA

Words by
RAFAEL NÚÑEZ (1825 - 1894)*

Music by
ORESTE SINDICI (1837 - 1904)

Officially adopted on 4 July, 1946. First sung on 11 November, 1887 in Bogota. There are eleven verses.
*Rafael Núñez was elected President of Colombia four times.

D.C. al Fine

pren - de las pa-la - bras Del que mu-rió en la Cruz.

D.C. al Fine

39

2. *'Independencia' grita*
   El mundo americano;
   Se baña en sangre de héroes
   La tierra de Colón.
   Pero este gran principio:
   'El Rey no es soberano',
   Resuena, y los que sufren
   Bendicen su pasión.

   CHORUS

Translation

CHORUS
Oh unfading glory!
Oh immortal joy!
In furrows of pain
Good is already germinating.   } (twice)

1. The fearful night came to an end,
   Liberty sublime
   Is spreading the dawns
   Of its invincible light.
   The whole of humanity,
   Which is groaning under chains,
   Understands the words
   Of the One who died on the Cross.

   CHORUS

2. 'Independence' cries
   The American world;
   In heroes' blood is bathing
   The Land of Columbus.
   But this great principle:
   'The King is not sovereign',
   Resounds, and those who suffer
   Praise the passion in it.

   CHORUS

THE COMOROS
Udzima wa ya Masiwa
(The Union of the Great Islands)

Words by
SAID HACHIM SIDI ABDEREMANE (*b.* 1942)

Music by
KAMILDINE ABDALLAH (1943 - 1982) and
SAID HACHIM SIDI ABDEREMANE (*b.* 1942)
Arr. by W. L. REED

Adopted in 1978.

ya ma-si-wa ya-ri-le-ya Mo-la né a-ri sa-yi-di-ya

Na - ri-ké - ni ha ni-ya ri - vein-dzé uwa-ta - ni-ya

Ma-ha-ba ya di-ne na du - ni - ya. I béra -

ba ———— ya hu-vein-dzar ya ma - si - wa.

Au faîte le Drapeau flotte
Appelle à la Liberté totale.
La nation apparaît,
Force d'une même religion au sein des Comores.
Vivons dans l'amour réciproque dans nos îles.

Les Comoriens issue de même sang,
Nous embrassons la même idéologie réligieuse.
Les îles où nous sommes nés.
Les îles qui nous ont prodigués la bonne éducation.
Dieu y a apporté son aide.
Conservons notre unité pour l'amour de la patrie,
Amour pour la réligion
Et pour l'évolution.

Au faîte le Drapeau flotte
Depuis le 6 du mois de Juillet
La nation apparaît,
Les îles devenues souveraines;
Maore—N'Dzouani—Mouwali—et N'Gazidja.
Gardons notre amour pour les îles.

English Translation by Jan Knappert

The flag is flying,
Announcing complete independence;
The nation rises up
Because of the faith we have
In this our Comoria.

Let us always have devotion
To love our Great Islands.
We Comorians are of one blood,
We Comorians are of one faith.

On these Islands we were born,
These Islands brought us up.
May God always help us;
Let us always have the firm resolve
To love our fatherland,
Love our religion and the world.

The flag is flying.
From the Sixth of July
The Nation rises up;
Our Islands are lined up.
Maori and Anzuan, Moheli and Comore,
Let us always have devotion
To love our Great Islands.

CONGO
La Congolaise

Words by
LEVENT KIMBANGUI *

Music by
FRANÇAIS JACQUES TONDRA *
Arr. by HENRY COLEMAN

1. En ce jour le so-leil se lè-ve Et no-tre Con-go res-plen-dit. U-ne lon-gue nuit s'a-chè-ve, Un grand bon-heur a sur-gi. Chan-tons

Originally adopted in 1962, replaced in 1969 and restored on 10 June, 1991.

* Dates not yet available

CHORUS

té. Con - go - lais, de - bout fiè - re -
ment par - tout, Pro - cla - mons l'u - nion de no - tre na - tion, Ou - bli -
ons ce qui nous di - vi - se, so - yons plus u - nis que ja -

tous a - vec i - vres - se le chant de la li - ber -

mais, Vi - vons pour no - tre de - vi - se: U - ni -

té, tra - vail, pro - grès! Vi - vons pour no - tre de -

allargando (3a volta)

vi - se: U - ni - té, tra - vail, pro - grès!

allargando (3a volta)

2. *Des forêts jusqu'à la savanne,*
   Des savannes jusqu'à la mer,
   Un seul peuple, une seule âme,
   Un seul cœur, ardent et fier,
   Luttons tous, tant que nous sommes,
   Pour notre vieux pays noir.

   CHORUS

3. *Et s'il nous faut mourir, en somme*
   Qu'importe puisque nos enfants,
   Partout, pourront dire comme
   On triomphe en combattant,
   Et dans le moindre village
   Chantent sous nos trois couleurs.

   CHORUS

1. On this day the sun rises
   And our Congo stands resplendent.
   A long night is ended,
   A great happiness has come.
   Let us all, with wild joyfulness, sing
   The song of freedom.

   CHORUS
   Arise, Congolese, proud every man,
   Proclaim the unity of our nation.
   Let us forget what divides us
   And become more united than ever.
   Let us live our motto:
   Unity, work, progress.
   Let us live our motto:
   Unity, work, progress.

2. From the forest to the bush,
   From the bush to the ocean,
   One people, one soul,
   One heart, ardent and proud.
   Let us all fight, every one of us,
   For our old black country.

   CHORUS

3. And if we have to die,
   What does it really matter? Our children
   Everywhere will be able to say how
   Triumph comes through battle,
   And in the smallest village
   Sing beneath our three colours.

   CHORUS

COSTA RICA

Words by
JOSÉ MARÍA ZELEDÓN BRENES (1877 - 1949)

Music by
MANUEL MARÍA GUTIÉRREZ (1829 - 1887)

Allegro marziale

No - ble pa - tria tu her - mo - sa ban - de - ra Ex - pre-

sión de tu vi - da nos da: Ba - jo el lím - pi - do a - zul de tu

The music was adopted in 1853; the words were chosen as a result of a public competition in 1900.

cie - lo   Blan - ca y pu - ra des - can - sa   la paz.

En   la   lu - cha te - naz   de   fe - cun - da   la - bor   Que en - ro -

je - ce del hom - bre   la   faz,   Con - qui - sta - ron   tus

hi - jos,   la - brie - gos   sen - ci - llos,   E - ter - no   pres - ti - gio,   es - ti - ma y ho -

nor, E - ter - no pres - ti - gio, es - ti - ma y ho - nor.

¡Sal - ve, oh tie - rra gen - til! ¡Sal - ve, oh ma - dre de a-

mor! Cuan-do al - gu - no pre - ten - da tu glo - ria man-

char,____ Ve - rás a tu pue - blo, va - lien - te y vi-

Translation by T. M. Cartledge

Noble homeland, your beautiful flag
Expresses for us your life:
Under the limpid blue of your skies,
Peace reigns, white and pure.
In the tenacious battle of fruitful toil,
That brings a glow to men's faces,
Your sons, simple farm hands,
Gained eternal renown, esteem and honour. } (twice)
Hail, gentle country!
Hail, loving mother!
If anyone should attempt to besmirch your glory,
You will see your people, valiant and virile,
Exchange their rustic tools for weapons.
Hail, O homeland! Your prodigal soil
Gives us sweet sustenance and shelter.
Under the limpid blue of your sky,
May peaceful labour ever continue.

CROATIA

Words by
ANTUN MIHANOVIĆ (1796 - 1861)

Music by
JOSIP RUNJANIN (1821 - 1878)
Arr. by W. L. REED

1. Lije - pa na - ša do - mo - vi - no, Oj ju - na - čka ze - mljo mi - la,

Sta - re sla - ve dje do - vi - no, Da bi va — zda sre - tna bi - la!

Mi - la, ka - no si nam— sla - vna, Mi - la si nam ti je - di - na.

Adopted on 22 December, 1990. Croatia achieved independence on 15 January, 1992.

Mi - la, ku - da si nam ra - vna, Mi - la, ku - da si pla - ni - na!

13

2. *Te cí Dravo, Savo teci,*
   Nit' ti Dunav silu gubi,
   Sinje more svijetu reci,
   Da svoj narod Hrvat ljubi.
   Dok mu njive sunce grije,
   Dok mu hrašcé bura vije,
   Dok mu mrtve grobak krije,
   Dok mu živo srce bije!

Translation

1. Our beautiful homeland,
   Oh dear, heroic land,
   Fatherland of ancient glory,
   May you always be happy!
   Dear, as much as you are glorious,
   Only you are dear to us.
   Dear, where your land is flat,
   Dear, where it is mountainous.

2. Flow Drava, Sava flow,
   Nor you, Danube, lose your power,
   Azure sea, tell to the world
   That a Croat loves his nation.
   As long as sun warms his ploughed land,
   As long as storms lash his oak trees,
   As long as the grave hides his dead,
   As long as his living heart beats!

CUBA
La Bayamesa
(The Bayamo Song)

Words and music by
PEDRO FIGUEREDO (1819 - 1870)

Sung for the first time in 1868 during the battle of Bayamo, in which Figueredo played a leading part.

me - ses, Que la Patria os contempla or - gu-
llo - sa; No temáis una muerte glorio -
sa, Que morir por la Patria es vivir._____ En ca-
de - nas vivir, es vivir_____ En a-

Translation by T. M. Cartledge

Hasten to battle, men of Bayamo,
For the homeland looks proudly to you.
You do not fear a glorious death,
Because to die for the country is to live.
To live in chains
Is to live in dishonour and ignominy. } (twice)
Hear the clarion call,
Hasten, brave ones, to battle!

CYPRUS

Words by
DIONYSIOS SOLOMÓS (1798 - 1857)

Music by
NIKOLAOS MANTZAROS (1795 - 1873)

Adopted when the Republic of Cyprus achieved independence in 1960. The National Anthem of Cyprus is the same as that of Greece.

prot' an - thri - o - me - ni hai - re o hai - r'e - lef - the - ria.___

22

English versification by T. M. Cartledge

I shall always recognise you
By the dreadful sword you hold,
As the earth, with searching vision,
You survey, with spirit bold.
'Twas the Greeks of old whose dying
Brought to birth our spirit free.
Now, with ancient valour rising,
Let us hail you, oh Liberty! } (three times)

CZECH REPUBLIC

Words by
JOSEF KAJETÁN TYL (1808 - 1856)

Music by
FRANTIŠEK JAN ŠKROUP (1801 - 1862)

1. Kde do-mov můj, kde do-mov můj? Vo-da hu-čí po lu-či-nách, bo-ry šu-mi po ska-li-nách, v sa-dě skvi——— se ja-ra květ, zem-ský

The State hymn of Czechoslovakia was composed in 1834, and officially recognised as the National Anthem in 1919. It was in two sections - Czech and Slovak. The Czech section has been retained by the new Czech Republic as the National Anthem. When Slovakia separated from the rest of the country on 1 January, 1993, she retained the Slovak section as her National Anthem.

ráj____ to na po - hled! A to je ta krá - sná ze - mě, ze - mě

če - ská, do - mov můj,— ze - mě če - ská, do - mov můj!

Translation

2. *Kde domov můj, kde domov můj?*
   V kraji znáš-li bohumilém,
   Duše útlé v těle čilém,
   Mysl jasnou, znik a zdar,
   A tu sílu, vzdoru zmar.
   To je Čechů slavné plémě,
   Mezi Čechy domov můj,
   Mezi Čechy domuv můj.

1. Where is my home, where is my home?
   Water bubbles across the meadows,
   Pinewoods rustle among crags,
   The garden is glorious with spring blossom,
   Paradise on earth it is to see.
   And this is that beautiful land,
   The Czech land, my home,
   The Czech land, my home.

2. Where is my home, where is my home?
   If, in a heavenly land, you have met
   Tender souls in agile frames,
   Of clear mind, vigorous and prospering,
   And with a strength that frustrates all defiance,
   That is the glorious race of the Czechs,
   Among Czechs (is) my home,
   Among Czechs, my home.

DENMARK

Words by
ADAM GOTTLOB OEHLENSCHLÄGER (1779 - 1850)

Music by
HANS ERNST KRØYER (1798 - 1879)
Arr. by W. L. REED

Words written in 1820. Its popularity as a National Anthem dates from 4 July, 1844, when students sang it at a national festival meeting to a gathering of 12,000 Danes. There are twelve verses. The National Anthem of Denmark is also used in the Faroe Islands and Greenland.

Denmark also has a Royal Anthem with words by Johannes Ewald (1743 - 1781) and music by Ditlev Ludvig Rogert (1742-1813) (see NATIONAL ANTHEMS OF THE WORLD – 5th EDITION).

2. *Der sad i fordums tid*
   De harnisk klædte kæmper,
   Udhvilede fra strid;
   Udhvilede fra strid;
   Så drog de frem til fjenders men,
   Nu hvile deres bene
   Bag højens bautasten,
   Bag højens bautasten.

3. *Det land endnu er skønt,*
   Thi blå sig søen bælter,
   Og løvet står så grønt;
   Og løvet står så grønt;
   Og ædle kvinder, skønne mø'r
   Og mænd og raske svende
   Bebo de danskes øer,
   Bebo de danskes øer.

Translation by R. P. Keigwin

2. There sat that earlier day
   The heroes in their harness
   And rested from the fray;
   And rested from the fray;
   Then forth they went, the foe they downed,
   But now their bones are resting
   'Neath bauta-stone and mound,
   'Neath bauta-stone and mound.

3. And still that land is fair,
   So blue the seas that belt her,
   So green the woodland there;
   So green the woodland there;
   And noble women, comely girls
   And men and lads of mettle
   Dwell in the Danish isles,
   Dwell in the Danish isles.

DJIBOUTI

Words by
ADEN ELMI (*b.* 1950)

Music by
ABDI ROBLEH (*b.* 1945)
Arr. by W. L. REED

Officially adopted in 1977.

Hinjinne u sara kaca
Calankaan harraad iyo
Haydaar u mudateen.

Hir cagaarku qariyayiyo
Habkay samadu tahayoo
Xiddig dhi igleh hoorshoo
Caddaan lagu hadheeyaay.

Maxaa haybad kugu yaal.

Translation

Arise with strength! For we have raised our flag,
The flag which has cost us dear
With extremes of thirst and pain.

Our flag, whose colours are the everlasting green of the earth,
The blue of the sky, and white, the colour of peace;
And in the centre the red star of blood.

Oh flag of ours, what a glorious sight !

DOMINICA

Words by
WILFRED OSCAR MORGAN POND (1912 - 1985)

Music by
LEMUEL McPHERSON CHRISTIAN (*b.* 1913)
Arr. by W. L. REED

1. Isle of beau - ty, isle of splen - dour, Isle to all so sweet and fair, All must sure - ly gaze in won - der At thy gifts so rich and

Originally adopted in 1967 on achieving Statehood, and again in 1978 when becoming independent.

2. Dominica, God hath blest thee
   With a clime benign and bright,
   Pastures green and flowers of beauty
   Filling all with pure delight,
   And a people strong and healthy,
   Full of godly, rev'rent fear.
   May we ever seek to praise Thee
   For these gifts so rich and rare.

3. Come ye forward, sons and daughters
   Of this gem beyond compare.
   Strive for honour, sons and daughters,
   Do the right, be firm, be fair.
   Toil with hearts and hands and voices.
   We must prosper! Sound the call,
   In which ev'ryone rejoices,
   "All for Each and Each for All."

DOMINICAN REPUBLIC

Words by
EMILIO PRUD'HOMME (1856 - 1932)

Music by
JOSÉ REYÉS (1835 - 1905)

1. *Quis - que - ya - nos va - lien - tes, al - ce - mos Nues - tro can - to con vi - va e - mo - ción, Y — del

Composed in 1883. First sung as National Anthem in 1900. There are six verses.
* Quisqueya is the native name of the island of Santo Domingo.

pió.

cresc. _dim._ _p_

_f_

2. Nin - gun pue - blo ser li - bre me-

_pp_ _f_

re - ce Si es es - cla - vo in do - len - te y ser - vil; Si en su

dim. _f_

pe - cho la lla - ma no cre - ce Que tem-

dim. _f_

Translation by T. M. Cartledge

1. Brave men of Quisqueya,
   Let us sing with strong feeling
   And let us show to the world
   Our invincible, glorious banner.
   Hail, O people who, strong and intrepid,
   Launched into war and went to death!
   Under a warlike menace of death,
   You broke your chains of slavery.

2. No country deserves to be free
   If it is an indolent and servile slave,
   If the call does not grow loud within it,
   Tempered by a virile heroism.
   But the brave and indomitable Quisqueya
   Will always hold its head high,
   For if it were a thousand times enslaved,
   It would a thousand times regain freedom.

ECUADOR

Words by
JUAN LEÓN MERA (1832 - 1894)*

Music by
ANTONIO NEUMANE (1818 - 1871)

Officially recognised by a government decree in 1948. It had been in use since 1865. There are six verses.
* Juan Mera in his later years was president of the Senate of Ecuador.

CHORUS

f Sal - ve, Oh Pa - tria, mil ve - ces! — ¡Oh

Pa - tria, Glo - ria a ti! Glo - ria a ti! Ya tu

pe - cho, tu pe - cho, — re - bo - sa Go - zo y paz ya tu pe - cho re -

174

bo - sa; Y tu fren - te,— tu fren - te ra - dio - sa Más que el

sol con - tem - pla - mos lu - cir,———— Y tu fren - te, tu fren - te ra-

dio sa Más que el sol con - tem - pla - mos lu -

ca - us - to Ye - sa san - gre fue ger - men fe-

cresc.

cun - do De o - tros hé - roes que a - tó - ni - to el

cresc.

mun - do Vió en tu tor - no a mi - lla - res sur-

1. *p*   2.   *f*

gir.   Dios mi - gir,   a mi - lla - res sur-

177

Translation by T. M. Cartledge

CHORUS

O homeland, we greet you a thousand times!
Glory be to you, O homeland, glory be to you!
Your breast overflows with joy and peace,
And we see your radiant face shining
More brightly than the sun.

The worthy sons of the soil
Which Pichincha on high is adorning,
Always acclaimed you as sovereign lady
And shed their blood for you.
God observed and accepted the sacrifice,
And that blood was the prolific seed
Of other heroes whom the world in astonishment saw
Arising in thousands around you.

} (twice)

CHORUS

EGYPT

Words and music by
SAYED DARWISH (1892 - 1923)
Arr. by W. L. REED

Adopted in 1979.

179

180

2. *Misr Inti Aghla Durra*
   Fawq Gabeen Ad-dahr Ghurra
   Ya Biladi 'Aishi Hurra
   Wa As 'Adi Raghm-al-adi.

   CHORUS

3. *Misr Awladik Kiram*
   Aufiya Yar'u-zimam
   Saufa Takhti Bil-maram
   Bittihadhim Wa-ittihadi.

   CHORUS

Translation

CHORUS
My homeland, my homeland, my homeland,
My love and my heart are for thee.
My homeland, my homeland, my homeland,
My love and my heart are for thee.

1. Egypt! O mother of all lands,
   My hope and my ambition,
   How can one count
   The blessings of the Nile for mankind?

   CHORUS

2. Egypt! Most precious jewel,
   Shining on the brow of eternity!
   O my homeland, be for ever free,
   Safe from every foe!

   CHORUS

3. Egypt! Noble are thy children,
   Loyal, and guardians of thy soil.
   In war and peace
   We give our lives for thy sake.

   CHORUS

EL SALVADOR

Words by
JUAN JOSÉ CAÑAS (1826 - 1918)

Music by
JUAN ABERLE (1846 - 1930)

Written in 1879 and adopted in 1953.

can - so a su bien__ con - sa - grar,

con __ sa - grar,

con __ sa - grar, con - sa -

grar, con - sa - grar.__

1. De la paz en la di - cha su-
pre - ma Siem - pre no - ble so - ñó El Sal - va-
dor. Fué ob - te - ner la su e - ter - no pro-
ble - ma, Con - ser - var - la es su glo - ria ma-

tad! _____ *es - cri - bió* _____ *li - ber -*

tad! _____ *es - cri - bió* _____ *li - ber - tad!*

D.C. al Fine

D.C. al Fine

56

57

189

CHORUS
Saludemos la patria orgullosos
De hijos suyos podernos llamar;
Y juremos la vida animosos,
Sin descanso a su bien consagrar.

2. *Libertad es su dogma, es su guía,*
   Que mil veces logró defender;
   Y otras tantas de audaz tirania
   Rechazar el odioso poder.
   Dolorosa y sangrienta es su historia,
   Pero excelsa y brillante a la vez,
   Manantial de legitima gloria,
   Gran lección de espartana altivez.
   No desmaya su innata bravura:
   En cada hombre hay un héroe inmortal,
   Que sabrá mantenerse a la altura
   De su antiguo valor proverbial.

   CHORUS

3. *Todos son abnegados y fieles*
   Al prestigio del bélico ardor,
   Con que siempre segaron laureles
   De la Patria salvando el honor.
   Respetar los derechos extraños
   Y apoyarse en la recta razón
   Es para ella, sin torpes amaños,
   La invariable, más firme ambición.
   Y en seguir esta línea se aferra,
   Dedicando su esfuerzo tenaz
   En hacer cruda guerra a la guerra;
   Su ventura se encuentra en la paz.

   CHORUS

Translation by T. M. Cartledge

CHORUS

Let us salute the motherland,
Proud to be called her children.
To her well-being let us swear
Boldly and unceasingly to devote our lives.

} (twice)

1. Of peace enjoyed in perfect happiness,
   El Salvador has always nobly dreamed.
   To achieve this has been her eternal proposition,
   To keep it, her greatest glory.
   With inviolable faith, she eagerly follows
   The way of progress
   In order to fulfil her high destiny
   And acheive a happy future.
   A stern barrier protects her
   Against the clash of vile disloyalty,
   Ever since the day when her lofty banner,
   In letters of blood, wrote "Freedom,"
   Wrote "Freedom," wrote "Freedom."

   CHORUS

2. Freedom is her dogma and her guide;
   A thousand times she has defended it,
   And as many times has she repelled
   The hateful power of atrocious tyranny.
   Her history has been bloody and sad,
   Yet at the same time sublime and brilliant,
   A source of legitimate glory
   And a great lesson in Spartan pride.
   Her innate bravery shall not waver:
   In every man there is an immortal hero
   Who knows how to maintain the level
   Of the proverbial valour of old.

   CHORUS

3. All are self-denying and faithful
   To the tradition of warlike ardour
   With which they have always reaped fame
   By saving the motherland's honour.
   To respect the rights of others
   And base her actions on right and justice
   Is for her, without infamous intrigue,
   The constant and most firm ambition.
   And in following this line she persists,
   Dedicating her tenacious efforts
   In giving hard battle for battle;
   Her happiness is found in peace.

   CHORUS

EQUATORIAL GUINEA

Words by
ATANASIO NDONGO MIYONO * (

Composer unknown
Arr. by W. L. REED

Ca - mi - ne - mos pi - san - do las sen - das De nuestra
in - men - sa fe - li - ci - dad. En fra - ter - ni - dad,
sin se - pa - ra - ción,— ¡Can - te - mos Li - ber - tad! Tras dos

Adopted in 1968, year of independence.
*Date of birth unknown.

siem - pre, Li - bre Gui - ne - a, Y con - ser - ve - mos siem - pre la u - ni -

tad. ¡Gri - ta - mos Vi - va, Li - bra Gui - ne - a, Y de - fen -

da - mos nues - tra Li - ber - tad. Can - te - mos siem - pre, Li - bre Gui -

ne - a,___ Y con - ser - ve - mos, Y con - ser - ve - mos La in - de - pen -

den - cia   na - cio - nal,   Y con - ser - ve - mos,   Y con - ser-

ve - mos   La in - de - pen - den - cia   na - cio - nal.

Let us tread the paths
Of our great happiness.
In brotherhood, undivided,
Let us sing for freedom!
Behind us are two centuries
Of colonial domination.
In brotherly unity, without discrimination,
Let us sing for freedom!
Let us shout: Long live Guinea!
Let us defend our freedom.
Always singing of our free Guinea,
Let us keep united.
Let us shout: Long live Guinea!
Let us defend our freedom.
Always singing of our free Guinea,
Let us keep our nation independent,
Let us keep our nation independent.

ERITREA

Words by
SOLOMON TSEHAYE BERAKI (*b.* 1956)

Music by
ISAAC ABRAHAM MEHAREZGHI (*b.* 1944)
and ARON TEKLE TESFATSION (*b.* 1963)
Arr. by ELIAS W. GABRIEL G. MICHAEL

Adopted on 19 May, 1993.

Translation

1. Eritrea, Eritrea, Eritrea,
   Her enemy decimated
   And her sacrifices vindicated by liberation.

2. Steadfast in her goal,
   Symbolising endurance,
   Eritrea, the pride of her oppressed people,
   Proved that the truth prevails.

   CHORUS
   Eritrea, Eritrea
   Holds her rightful place in the world.

ESTONIA

Words by
JOHANN VOLDEMAR JANNSEN (1819 - 1900)

Music by
FRIEDRICH PACIUS (1809 - 1891)
Arr. by HENRY COLEMAN

1. Mu i - sa - maa, mu õnn ja rõõm, Kui kau - nis o - led sa! Ei lei - a mi - na— ii - al teal See suu - re lai - a— il - ma peal, Mis

Sung publicly for the first time at the First Estonian National Song Festival in Tartu on 1 July, 1869. The melody though shorter is the same as that of the National Anthem of Finland.

199

mull' nii ar - mas o - leks ka   Kui   sa   mu i - sa - maa!

2. *Sa oled mind ju sünnitand*
   Ja üles kasvatand;
   Sind tänan mina alati
   Ja jään sul truuks surmani!
   Mul kõige armsam oled sa,
   Mu kallis isamaa!

3. *Su üle Jumal valvaku,*
   Mu armas isamaa!
   Ta olgu sinu kaitseja
   Ja võtku rohkest' õnnista'
   Mis iial ette võtad sa,
   Mu kallis isamaa!

Translation by Jenny Wahl

1. My native land, my joy, delight,
   How fair thou art and bright!
   And nowhere in the world all round
   Can ever such a place be found
   So well beloved as I love thee,
   My native country dear!

2. My little cradle stood on thy soil,
   Whose blessings ease my toil.
   With my last breath my thanks to thee,
   For true to death I'll ever be,
   O worthy, most beloved and fine,
   Thou, dearest country mine!

3. May God in Heaven thee defend,
   My best, my dearest land!
   May He be guard, may He be shield,
   For ever may He bless and wield
   O graciously all deeds of thine,
   Thou dearest country mine!

ETHIOPIA

Words by
DEREJE MELAKU MENGESHA (*b.* 1957)

Music by
SOLOMON LULU MITIKU (*b.* 1950)
Arr. by W. L. REED

Adopted in 1992.

Yäzêgennät Keber Bä-Ityopp'yachchen S'änto
Tayyä Hezbawinnät Dar Eskädar Bürlo.
Läsälam Läfeteh Lühezboch Näs'annät;
Bä'ekkulennät Bäfeqer Qomänal Bä'andennät.
Mäsärätä S'enu Säbe'enan Yalsharen;
Hezboch Nän Läsera Bäsera Yänoren.
Denq Yäbahel Mädräk Yä'akuri Qers Baläbet;
Yätäfät'ro S'ägga Yäjägna Hezb Ennat.
Ennet'äbbeqeshallän Alläbben Adära;
Ityopp'yachchen nuri Eññam Banchi Ennekura!

Transliteration and translation by D. L. Appleyard

Respect for citizenship is strong in our Ethiopia;
National pride is seen, shining from one side to another.
For peace, for justice, for the freedom of peoples,
In equality and in love we stand united.
Firm of foundation, we do not dismiss humanness;
We are peoples who live through work.
Wonderful is the stage of tradition, mistress of proud heritage,
Mother of natural virtue, mother of a valorous people.
We shall protect you - we have a duty;
Our Ethiopia, live! And let us be proud of you!

FIJI

Words by
MICHAEL FRANCIS ALEXANDER PRESCOTT (*b.* 1928)

Composer unknown*
Arr. by W. L. REED

1. Bless - ing grant, oh God of na - tions, on the isles of Fi - ji,

As we stand u - ni - ted un - der no - ble ban - ner blue.

And we hon - our and de - fend the cause of free - dom e - ver,

*The melody is based on an old traditional Fijian song.
Fiji became independent on 10 October, 1970.

Fi - ji, for ev - er - more!

2. Blessing grant, oh God of nations, on the isles of Fiji,
   Shores of golden sand and sunshine, happiness and song.
   Stand united, we of Fiji, fame and glory ever,
   Onward march together, God bless Fiji!

   CHORUS

FINLAND

Original Swedish words by
JOHAN LUDVIG RUNEBERG (1804 - 1877)
Finnish words by
PAAVO EEMIL CAJANDER (1846 - 1913)

Music by
FREDRIK PACIUS (1809 - 1891)

Andante maestoso

1. Oi Maam - me, Suo - mi, syn - nyin - maa! Soi sa - na kul - tai - nen! Ei laak - so - a,— ei— kuk - ku - laa, Ei vet - tä, ran - taa— rak- kaam-paa, Kuin

The words were written in 1846. Sung for the first time at a student's gathering on 13 May, 1848. The melody is the same as that of the National Anthem of Estonia.

ko - ti - maa tää poh - joi - nen, Maa kal - lis i - si - en!

11

2. Sun kukoistukses kuorestaan
   Kerrankin puhkeaa!
   Viel' lempemme saa nousemaan
   Sun toivos, riemus loistossaan,
   Ja kerran laulus, synnyinmaa,
   Korkeemman kaiun saa!

Swedish

Translation by Charles Wharton Stork

1. Vårt land, vårt land, vårt fosterland,
   Ljud högt, o dyra ord!
   Ej lyfts en höjd mot himlens rand,
   Ej sänks en dal, ej sköljs en strand,
   Mer älskad än vår bygd i nord,
   Än våra fäders jord.

2. Din blomning, sluten än i knopp,
   Skall mogna ur sitt tvång;
   Se, ur vår kärlek skall gå opp
   Ditt ljus, din glans, din fröjd, ditt hopp,
   Och högra klinga skall en gång
   Vår fosterländska sång.

1. Our land, our land, our native land,
   Oh, let her name ring clear!
   No peaks against the heavens that stand,
   No gentle dales or foaming strand
   Are loved as we our home revere,
   The earth our sires held dear.

2. The flowers in their buds that grope
   Shall burst their sheaths with spring;
   So from our love to bloom shall ope
   Thy gleam, thy glow, thy joy, thy hope,
   And higher yet some day shall ring
   The patriot song we sing!

FRANCE
La Marseillaise

Words and music by
CLAUDE-JOSEPH ROUGET DE L'ISLE (1760 - 1836)

1. Al - lons en - fants de la Pa - tri - e, Le jour de gloire est ar - ri - vé. Con - tre nous, de la ty - ran - ni - e, L'é - ten - dard sang - lant est le - vé, l'e - ten-

Written and composed on 24 April, 1792, as a marching song. Adopted as the National Anthem on 15 July, 1795.
The National Anthem of France is also used in French Guiana, French Polynesia, Guadeloupe, Martinique, Mayotte, New Caledonia, Réunion, St. Pierre-Miquelon and Wallis & Futuna Islands.

dard—— sang-lant est le - vé. En - ten - dez - vous, dans les cam-

pag - nes Mu — gir ces fa-rou - ches sol - dats. Ils

vien - nent jus-que dans nos bras é - gor - ger vos fils,—— vos com-

pag - nes. Aux ar — mes ci - toy-ens! For-

*This part of the Anthem is generally repeated

210

mez____ vos ba-tail-lons,____ Mar-chons, mar-chons!

Qu'un sang im-pur____ A-breu - ve nos sil-lons.

2. Amour sacré de la Patrie,
   Conduis, soutiens nos bras vengeurs.
   Liberté, liberté chérie,
   Combats avec tes défenseurs; } (twice)
   Sous nos drapeaux, que la victoire
   Accoure à tes mâles accents;
   Que tes ennemis expirants
   Voient ton triomphe et notre glorie!
   Aux armes citoyens! etc.

Translation by T. M. Cartledge

1. Arise, children of the fatherland,
   The day of glory has come.
   Against us the blood-stained banner
   Of tyranny is raised,
   The banner of tyranny is raised,
   Hear, in the fields, the roar
   Of her fierce soldiers.
   They come right into our arms
   To slaughter our sons and our consorts.
   Patriots, to arms!
   Form your battalions,
   Let's march, let's march!
   May the tyrant's foul blood water our furrows!

2. Sacred love of country,
   May you guide and sustain our avenging hands.
   Freedom, dear freedom,
   Fight along with those who defend you,
   Fight along with those who defend you.
   Under our flags, may victory
   Follow your manly accents;
   May your dying enemies
   See your triumph and our glory!
   Patriots, to arms!
   Form your battalions,
   Let's march, let's march!
   May the tyrant's foul blood water our furrows!

GABON

Words and music by
GEORGES ALEKA DAMAS (1902 - 1982)
Arr. by HENRY COLEMAN

Tempo di marcia
CHORUS

U - ni⎯ dans la Con - cor - de et la⎯ fra - ter - ni - té,⎯ E - veil - le - toi Ga - bon, une au - ro - re se lè - ve, En - cou - ra - ge l'ar - deur qui

This became the National Anthem upon independence on 17 August, 1960.
© Copyright 1960 by Henry Lemoine & Cie. 17 rue Pigalle, Paris.

vibre et nous sou - lè - ve!___ C'est en - fin notre es - sor vers la fé -

li - ci - té. C'est en - fin notre es - sor vers la fé - li - ci - té.

rall. 2nd time FINE

1. E - blou - is - sant et fier,___ le jour

p dolce

su - bli - me monte___ Pour - chas - sant à ja - mais___

l'in - jus - tice et la hon - te. Qu'il mon -

te, monte en - co - re et cal - me nos a -

lar - mes, Qu'il prô - ne la ver - tu_____

et re - pous - se les armes._____ U -

CHORUS

D. 𝄋

D. 𝄋

214

2. *Oui que le temps heureux rêvé par nos ancêtres*
   Arrive enfin chez nous, rejouisse les êtres,
   Et chasse les sorciers, ces perfides trompeurs
   Qui semaient le poison et répandaient la peur.

   CHORUS

3. *Afin qu'aux yeux du monde et des nations amies*
   Le Gabon immortel reste digne d'envie,
   Oublions nos querelles, ensemble bâtissons
   L'édifice nouveau auquel tous nous rêvons.

   CHORUS

4. *Des bords de l'Océan au cœur de la forêt,*
   Demeurons vigilants, sans faiblesse et sans haine!
   Autour de ce drapeau, qui vers l'honneur nous mène,
   Saluons la Patrie et chantons sans arrêt:

   CHORUS

Translation by T. M. Cartledge

CHORUS
United in concord and brotherhood,
Awake, Gabon, dawn is at hand.
Stir up the spirit that thrills and inspires us!
At last we rise up to attain happiness.

1. Dazzling and proud, the sublime day dawns,
   Dispelling for ever injustice and shame.
   May it still advance and calm our fears,
   May it promote virtue and banish warfare.

   CHORUS

2. Yes, may the happy days of which our ancestors dreamed
   Come for us at last, rejoicing our hearts,
   And banish the sorcerers, those perfidious deceivers
   Who sowed poison and spread fear.

   CHORUS

3. So that, in the eyes of the world and of friendly nations,
   The immortal Gabon may maintain her good repute,
   Let us forget our quarrels, let us build together
   The new structure of which we all have dreamed.

   CHORUS

4. From the shores of the Ocean to the heart of the forest,
   Let us remain vigilant, without weakness and without hatred!
   Around this flag which leads us to honour,
   Let us salute the Fatherland and ever sing:

   CHORUS

215

THE GAMBIA

Words by
VIRGINIA JULIE HOWE (*b.* 1927)

Adapted by
JEREMY FREDERICK HOWE (*b.* 1929)
from the traditional Mandinka song
'Foday Kaba Dumbuya'
Arr. by W. L. REED

For The Gam - bi - a, our— home - land, We— strive and work and pray, That— all may— live in u - ni - ty, Free - dom and peace each day. Let jus - tice guide our ac - tions To - wards the com - mon

Officially adopted on 18 February, 1965, when the country became independent.

GEORGIA

Words and Music by
KOTE POTSKHVERASHVILI (1889 - 1959)
Arr. by W. L. REED

1. Di - de - ba zet - sit kurt - he - uls, Di - de - ba kveh - nad sa - mot - khes, Tur - pha i - ver - sa.

Di - de - ba dzmo - bas, er - to - bas.

Officially adopted in 1991.

Di - de - ba ta - vi - su - ple - bas,
Di - de - ba sa -

rit. e cresc.

ma - ra - di - so Kar - tul - mkhne__ er - sa!

rit. e cresc.

2. *Dideba chvensa samshoblos,*
   Dideba chveni sitsotskhlis,
   Mizans diadsa;
   Vasha lrphobusu, sikvaruls,
   Vasha shvebasa, siharuls,
   Salami cheshmaritebis,
   Shuk gantiadsa!

Translation by Akaki Beruchashvili and Tamara Dragadze

1. Praise be to the heavenly Bestower of Blessings,
   Praise be to paradise on earth,
   To the radiant Iberians*,
   Praise be to brotherhood and to unity,
   Praise be to liberty,
   Praise be to the everlasting, lively Georgian people!

2. Praise be to our fatherland,
   Praise be to the great and bright aim of our lives;
   Hail, O joy and love,
   Hail helpfulness and happiness,
   Greetings to the truth, that light of dawn!

   * An alternative name for the Georgians.

GERMANY

Words by
AUGUST HEINRICH HOFFMANN VON FALLERSLEBEN (1798 - 1874)

Music by
FRANZ JOSEPH HAYDN (1732 - 1809)

Maestoso

Ein - ig - keit und Recht und Frei - heit Für das

deut - sche Va - ter - land! Da - nach lasst uns al - le

stre - ben Brü - der - lich mit Herz und— Hand! Ein - ig -

Authorised on 11 August, 1922, when the first verse of von Fallersleben's poem was sung. In 1952 the Federal Republic adopted the third verse instead as the official words. The re-unification of West and East Germany took place on 3 October, 1990. The National Anthem of West Germany was retained.

Translation

Unity and Right and Freedom
For the German Fatherland!
After these let us all strive
Brotherly with heart and hand!
Unity and Right and Freedom
Are the pledge of happiness.
Bloom in the splendour of this happiness,   } (twice)
Bloom, my German Fatherland!

GHANA

Words by the
GHANA GOVERNMENT

Music by
PHILIP GBEHO (1905 - 1976)
Arr. by W. L. REED

1. God bless our home - land Gha - na____ And make our na - tion great and strong,____ Bold to de - fend for ev - er____ The

Officially became the National Anthem in 1957, the year when independence was attained. The original words were written in 1956, as was the music, but replaced by the present text following a change of government in 1966.

cause of Free - dom and— of Right;_____ Fill__ our

hearts with__ true hu - mil - i - ty, Make__ us

cher - ish__ fear - less hon - es - ty,_____ And

help us to re - sist op - pres - sor's rule With all our

will and might— for ev - er-more.———— And more.————

2. Hail to thy name, O Ghana,
   To thee we make our solemn vow:
   Steadfast to build together
   A nation strong in Unity;
   With our gifts of mind and strength of arm,
   Whether night or day, in mist or storm,
   In ev'ry need, whate'er the call may be,
   To serve thee, Ghana, now and evermore. } (twice)

3. Raise high the flag of Ghana
   And one with Africa advance;
   Black Star of hope and honour
   To all who thirst for Liberty;
   Where the banner of Ghana freely flies,
   May the way to freedom truly lie;
   Arise, arise, O sons of Ghanaland,
   And under God march on for evermore! } (twice)

GIBRALTAR

Words and music by
PETER EMBERLEY (*b.* 1955)
Arr. by BARRIE HINGLEY and W. L. REED

Gib - ral - tar, Gib - ral - tar, the rock on which I — stand.

May you be for - ev - er free, Gib - ral - tar, my own land.

Might - y pil - lar, rock of splen - dour, guard - ian of the sea.

Chosen as a result of a competition and officially adopted on 18 October, 1994.

Port of hope in times of need, rich—— in hist-o—ry. Gib-

ral—tar, Gib-ral—tar, the rock on which I—— stand,

May you be for-ev-er free, Gib-ral—tar, my own land.

God give grace to this our home-land, help us to live as one.

Strong in freed - om, truth and just - ice, let___ this be our

song; Gib - ral - tar, Gib - ral - tar, the rock on which I___

stand, May you be for - ev - er free, Gib -

ral - tar!___ Gib - ral - tar! my own land.

GREECE
Imnos Eis Tin Eleftherian
(Hymn To Freedom)

Words by
DIONYSIOS SOLOMÓS (1798 - 1857)

Music by
NIKOLAOS MANTZAROS (1795 - 1873)

Maestoso

Se - gno - ri - so a - po tin Kop - si tou spa-

thiou tin tro - me - ri;_____ Se - gno - ri - so a - po tin

op - si pou me via me - tra tin yi._____ Ap ta

Chosen by King George I and adopted in 1864. There are one hundred and fifty eight verses. The National Anthem of Greece is the same as that of Cyprus.

Kok - ka - la vyal - me - ni ton el - li - non ta ie -

ra_____ Ke san prot' an - thri - o - me - ni hai - re o

hai - r'e - lef - the - ria._____ Ke san prot' an thri - o -

me - ni hai - re o hai - r'e - lef - the - ria,_____ Ke san

prot' an - thri - o - me - ni hai - re o hai - r'e - lef - the - ria.___

22

English versification by T. M. Cartledge

I shall always recognise you
By the dreadful sword you hold,
As the earth, with searching vision,
You survey, with spirit bold.
'Twas the Greeks of old whose dying
Brought to birth our spirit free.
Now, with ancient valour rising,
Let us hail you, oh Liberty!   } (three times)

GRENADA

Words by
IRVA MERLE BAPTISTE (*b.* 1924)

Music by
LOUIS ARNOLD MASANTO (*b.* 1938)

Hail! Gre na - da, land of ours, We pledge our - selves to thee, Heads, hearts and hands in u - ni - ty To

Officially adopted on Independence Day, 7 February, 1974.

reach our des - ti - ny. Ev - er con - scious of God, Be - ing

proud of our her - it - age, May we with faith and

cour - age As - pire,___ build, ad - vance As one

peo - ple, one fam - i - ly. God bless our na - tion.

GUATEMALA

Words by
JOSÉ JOAQUÍN PALMA (1844 - 1911)

Music by
RAFAEL ALVAREZ OVALLE (1860 - 1948)

Chosen from entries in a public competition in 1887. Adopted by governmental decrees of 28 October, 1896 and 19 February, 1897, and modified by decree of 26 July, 1934. There are four verses.

fie - ra An - tes muer - to q'_es - cla - vo se - rá.

36

Translation by T. M. Cartledge

VERSE
Fortunate Guatemala! May your altars
Never be profaned by cruel men.
May there never be slaves who submit to their yoke,
Or tyrants who deride you.
If tomorrow your sacred soil
Should be threatened by foreign invasion,
Your fair flag, flying freely in the wind,
Will call to you: Conquer or die.

CHORUS
Your fair flag, flying freely in the wind,
Will call to you: Conquer or die;
For your people, with heart and soul,
Would prefer death to slavery.

GUINEA

Author unknown

Music by
FODEBA KEITA (1925 - 1970)

Guinea became independent on 2 October, 1958.

Peuple d'Afrique!
Le Passé historique!
Que chante l'hymne de la Guinée fière et jeune -
Illustre epopée de nos frères
Morts au champ d'honneur en libérant l'Afrique!
Le peuple de Guinée prêchant l'unité
Appelle l'Afrique.
Liberté! C'est la voix d'un peuple
Qui appelle tous ses frères a se retrouver.
Liberté! C'est la voix d'un peuple
Qui appelle tous ses frères de la grande Afrique.
Bâtissons l'unité africaine dans l'indépendance retrouvée.

Translation

People of Africa!
The historic past!
Sing the hymn of a Guinea proud and young -
Illustrious epic of our brothers
Who died on the field of honour while liberating Africa!
The people of Guinea, preaching Unity,
Call to Africa.
Liberty! The voice of a people
Who call all her brothers to find their way again.
Liberty! The voice of a people
Who call all her brothers of a great Africa.
Let us build African Unity in a newly found independence!

GUINEA - BISSAU

Words and music by
AMILCAR LOPES CABRAL (1924 - 1973)

Allegro moderato, alla marcia

1. Sol, su - or e o ver - de e mar, Sé - cu - los de dor e es - peran - ça: Es - ta é a ter - ra dos

Composed in 1963. Adopted on Independence Day, 24 September, 1974. This National Anthem is the same as that of Cape Verde.

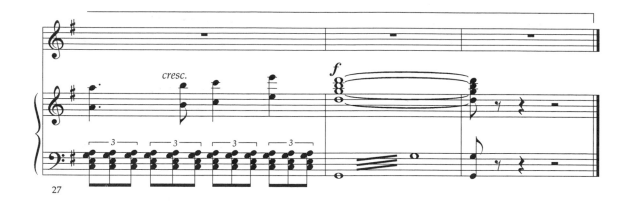

27

2. *Ramos do mesmo tronco,*
   Olhos na mesma luz:
   Esta é a força da nossa união!
   Cantem o mar e a terra
   A madrugada eo sol
   Que a nossa luta fecundou.

   CHORUS

Translation

1. Sun, sweat, verdure and sea,
   Centuries of pain and hope;
   This is the land of our ancestors.
   Fruit of our hands,
   Of the flower of our blood:
   This is our beloved country.

   CHORUS
   Long live our glorious country!
   The banner of our struggle
   Has fluttered in the skies.
   Forward, against the foreign yoke!
   We are going to build
   Peace and progress
   In our immortal country! } (twice)

2. Branches of the same trunk,
   Eyes in the same light;
   This is the force of our unity!
   The sea and the land,
   The dawn and the sun are singing
   That our struggle has borne fruit!

   CHORUS

GUYANA

Words by
ARCHIBALD LEONARD LUKER (1917 - 1971)

Music by
ROBERT CYRIL GLADSTONE POTTER (1899 - 1981)
Arr. by W. L. REED

1. Dear land of Guy-a-na, of ri-vers and plains; Made rich by the sun-shine and lush by the rains, Set gem-like and fair be-tween moun-tains and sea, Your

The words and music were selected as the result of a competition, and were approved by the House of Assembly on 21 April, 1966. Guyana became independent on 26 May, 1966.

child - ren sa - lute you, dear land_____ of the free.

2. Green land of Guyana, our heroes of yore,
   Both bondsmen and free, laid their bones on your shore.
   This soil so they hallowed, and from them are we,
   All sons of one Mother, Guyana the free.

3. Great land of Guyana, diverse through our strains,
   We are born of their sacrifice, heirs of their pains,
   And ours is the glory their eyes did not see -
   One land of six peoples, united and free.

4. Dear land of Guyana, to you will we give
   Our homage, our service, each day that we live;
   God guard you, great Mother, and make us to be
   More worthy our heritage- land of the free.

HAITI
La Dessalinienne
(The Dessalines Song)

Words by
JUSTIN LHÉRISSON (1873 - 1907)

Music by
NICOLAS GEFFRARD (1871 - 1930)

Allegro moderato - Tempo di marcia

1. Pour le Pa - ys, Pour la Pa - tri - e, Mar - chons u -
nis, Mar - chons u - nis. Dans nos rangs point de
traî - tres! Du sol soy - ons seuls maî - tres. Pour le Pa -

Composed for the centenary of national independence in 1904. The title is derived from Jean-Jacques Dessalines, the founder of Haiti as an independent republic.

2. *Pour les Aïeux,*
   Pour la Patrie
   Bêchons joyeux:
   Quand le champ fructifie
   L'âme se fortifie.
   Bêchons joyeux
   Pour les Aïeux,
   Pour la Patrie.

3. *Pour le Pays*
   Et pour nos Pères
   Formons des Fils.
   Libres, forts et prospères,
   Toujours: nous serons frères,
   Formons des fils
   Pour le Pays
   Et pour nos Pères.

4. *Pour les Aïeux,*
   Pour la Patrie
   O Dieu des Preux!
   Sous ta garde infinie
   Prends nos droits, notre vie,
   O Dieu des Preux!
   Pour les Aïeux,
   Pour la Patrie.

5. *Pour le Drapeau,*
   Pour la Patrie
   Mourir est beau!
   Notre passé nous crie:
   Ayez l'âme aguerrie!
   Mourir est beau
   Pour le Drapeau,
   Pour la Patrie.

Translation by T. M. Cartledge

1. For our country,
   For our forefathers,
   United let us march.
   Let there be no traitors in our ranks!
   Let us be masters of our soil.
   United let us march
   For our country,
   For our forefathers.

2. For our forebears,
   For our country
   Let us toil joyfully
   May the fields be fertile
   And our souls take courage.
   Let us toil joyfully
   For our forebears,
   For our country.

3. For our country
   And for our forefathers,
   Let us train our sons.
   Free, strong and prosperous,
   We shall always be as brothers.
   Let us train our sons
   For our country
   And for our forefathers.

4. For our forebears,
   For our country,
   Oh God of the valiant!
   Take our rights and our life
   Under your infinite protection,
   Oh God of the valiant!
   For our forebears,
   For our country.

5. For the flag,
   For our country
   To die is a fine thing!
   Our past cries out to us:
   Have a disciplined soul!
   To die is a fine thing,
   For the flag,
   For our country.

HONDURAS

Words by
AUGUSTO CONSTANCIO COELLO (1883 - 1941)

Music by
CARLOS HARTLING (1869 - 1920)

Tempo di marcia
con energia

Tu ban-de - ra, tu ban-de - ra Es un lam - po de cie-lo Por un blo - que, por un blo - que De— nie-ve cru - za-do; Y se

Selected as a result of a public competition, and adopted in 1915. There are six verses.

as - tro, hay un as - tro De__ ní - ti - da luz.

Meno mosso

FINE _p_ **VERSE**

1. *In - dia, vir - gen y her - mo - sa dor -*

mí - as De tus ma - res al can - to so - no - ro, Cuan - do e -

cha - da en tus cuen - cas de o - ro El au - daz na - ve - gan - te te ha -

250

lló; Y al mi - rar tu be - lle - za ex - ta - si - a - do Al in -

flu - jo i-de-al de tu en - can - to, La or - la a -

zul de tu es - plén - di - do____ man - to Con su

D.C. (al Fine after Verse 2)

be - so de a - mor con - sa - gró.

D.C. (al Fine after Verse 2)

2. *Por guardar ese emblema divino,*
   Marcharemos Oh Patria a la muerte,
   Generosa será nuestra suerte,
   Si morimos pensando en tu amor.
   Defendiendo tu santa bandera
   Y en tus pliegues gloriosos cubiertos,
   Serán muchos, Oh Honduras tus muertos,
   Pero todos caerán con honor.

   CHORUS

Translation by T. M. Cartledge

CHORUS
Your flag is a splendour of sky
Crossed with a band of snow;
And there can be seen, in its sacred depths,
Five pale blue stars.
In your emblem, which a rough sea
With its wild waves protects,
Behind the bare summit of a volcano,
A star brightly shines.

1. Like an Indian maiden you were sleeping,
   Lulled by the resonant song of your seas,
   When, set in your golden valleys,
   The bold navigator found you;
   And on seeing, enraptured, your beauty,
   And feeling your enchantment,
   He dedicated a kiss of love to the blue hem
   Of your splendid mantle.

   CHORUS

2. To guard this sacred emblem
   We shall march, oh fatherland, to our death;
   Our death will be honoured
   If we die thinking of your love.
   Having defended your holy flag,
   And shrouded in its glorious folds,
   Many, Honduras, shall die for you,
   But all shall fall in honour.

   CHORUS

HUNGARY

Words by
FERENC KÖLCSEY (1790 - 1838)

Music by
FERENC ERKEL (1810 - 1893)

Is - ten, áldd meg a ma - gyart Jó kedv - vel, bö - ség - gel,

Officially adopted in 1844. There are eight verses.
© Copyright 1959 by Zenemükiadó Vállalat, Budapest.

Nyújts fe - lé - je vé - dö kart, Ha küzd el - len -

ség - gel; Bal - sors a - kit ré - gen tép,

Hozz re - á vig esz - ten - döt, Meg - bün - höd - te

már e nép A múl - tat sjö - ven - döt.

Translation

God Bless the Hungarians
With good cheer and prosperity.
Extend a protective arm
If they fight the enemy.
Torn by misfortune for long,
Give them happy years.
These people have expiated
The past and the future.

ICELAND

Lofsöngur
(Song of Praise)

Words by
MATTHÍAS JOCHUMSSON (1835 - 1920)

Music by
SVEINBJÖRN SVEINBJÖRNSSON (1847 - 1926)
Arr. by W. L. REED

Ó, guð, vors lands, ó, lands vors guð, vjer lof - um þitt heil - ag - a,

heil - ag - a nafn. Úr sól - kerf - um himn - ann - a knýt - a þjer kranz þín - ir

her - skar - ar, tím - ann - a safn. Fyr - ir þjer er einn dag - ur sem

Written and composed in 1874, when Iceland secured its own constitution and also celebrated the one thousandth anniversary of the first permanent Norwegian settlers. There are three verses.

þús - und — ár, og þús - und ár dag - ur, ei meir, Eitt

ei - lifð - ar smá blóm með titr - and - i tár, sem til - bið - ur guð sinn og

deyr. Ís - lands þús und ár, Ís lands þús - und ár Eitt

ei - lifð - ar smá - blóm með titr - and - i tár, sem til - bið - ur guð sinn og deyr.

Translation by Nicholas Jones

O God of our land, O our land's God,
We worship Thy holy, holy name.
From the solar systems of the heavens bind for you a wreath
Your warriors, the assembly of the ages.
For Thee is one day as a thousand years,
And a thousand years a day and no more,
One small flower of eternity with a quivering tear,
That prays to its God and dies.
Iceland's thousand years, Iceland's thousand years,
One small flower of eternity with a quivering tear,
That prays to its God and dies.

INDIA

Words and music by
RABINDRANATH TAGORE (1861 - 1941) *
Arr. by SHIVA SHARAN (ALAIN DANIELOU)

First published 1912. Officially adopted by the Constitutional Assembly on 24 January, 1950, two days before the proclamation of the Republic. There are five verses in all. Only the first is usually sung.

*Rabindranath Tagore also wrote the words and music of the National Anthem of Bangladesh.

Ya - mu - nā,— Gan - gā, Uch' - chha - lă - ja - la - dhi - ta ran - gă.

Ta - va shu - bhă nā - mā sé ja - gé, Ta - va - shu - bhă ā - shī - shă

má - gé, ga - vé ta - vā ja - yā ga - thā.

Ja - nă - ga - nă - man - ga - lă - dă ya - kă, ja - yă he! Bhā - ra - tă - bhag - yă - vi -

260

he!   Ja - yă,   ja - yă,   ja - yă,   ja - yă   he!

Translation

1. Glory to thee, ruler of our hearts and of India's destiny!
   Punjab, Sind, Gujrat, Maharashtra,
   The land of the Dravids, Orissa, Bengal,
   The Vindhyas and Himalayas, the Jamuna
   And the Ganges and the ceaseless waves of the Ocean
   All arise at thy fair name and seek thy blessings,
   Singing their hymn of praise to thee.
   Glory to thee, Oh Goddess of India's fortune!
   Hail, hail, hail to thee for ever!

2. Day and night thy call spreads over the land
   And we hear thy voice of salvation,
   Hindus, Buddhists, Sikhs, Jains,
   Parsees, Muslims and Christians
   Come from East and West to the foot of thy throne,
   Singing their song of devotion to thee.
   Oh glory to thee, who unites our hearts and gives us good fortune!
   Hail, hail, hail to thee for ever!

INDONESIA

Words and music by
WAGE RUDOLF SOEPRATMAN (1903 - 1938)

Adopted as the Nationalist Party Song in 1928, and became the National Anthem in 1949.

lah ta-nah-ku, Hi-dup-lah ne-gri-ku, Bang-sa-ku, Rak-jat-ku se-'m-

wa - nja. Ba-ngun-lah ji-wa-nja, Ba-ngun-lah ba-dan-nja Un-tuk

CHORUS

In-do-ne-sia Ra-ja. In-do-ne-sia Ra-ja, Mer-de-

ka, Mer-de-ka, Ta-nah-ku ne-gri-ku jang ku-tjin - ta. In-do-

266

ne - sia Ra - ja, Mer - de - ka, Mer - de - ka, Hi - dup-

lah In - do-ne - sia Ra - ja.   In - do - ja.

2. Indonesia! Tanah jang mulia,
   Tanah kita jang kaja.
   Disanalah aku berada
   Untuk s'lamalamanja.
   Indonesia Tanah pusaka,
   P'saka Kita semuanja.
   Marilah kita mendo'a,
   "Indonesia bahagia!"
   Suburlah Tanahnja,
   Suburlah jiwanja,
   Bangsanja, Rakjatnja se'mwanja.
   Sadarlah hatinja,
   Sadarlah budinja
   Untuk Indonesia Raja.

   CHORUS

3. Indonesia! Tanah jang sutji,
   Tanah kita jang sakti.
   Disanalah aku berdiri
   'Ndjaga ibu sedjati.
   Indonesia Tanah berseri,
   Tanah jang aku sajangi.
   Mirilah kita berdjandji,
   "Indonesia abadi!"
   S'lamatlah Rakjatnja,
   S'lamatlah putranja,
   Pulaunja, lautnja se'mwanja.
   Madjulah Negrinja,
   Madjulah Pandunja
   Untuk Indonesia Raja.

   CHORUS

Translation

1. Indonesia, our native country,
   Our birthplace,
   Where we all arise to stand guard
   Over this our Motherland:
   Indonesia our nationality,
   Our people and our country.
   Come then, let us all exclaim
   Indonesia united.
   Long live our land,
   Long live our state,
   Our nation, our people, and all
   Arise then, its spirit,
   Arise, its bodies
   For Great Indonesia.

   CHORUS
   Indonesia the Great, independent and free,
   Our beloved country.
   Indonesia the Great, independent and free,
   Long live Indonesia the Great!

2. Indonesia, an eminent country,
   Our wealthy country,
   There we shall be forever.
   Indonesia, the country of our
         ancestors,
   A relic of all of us.
   Let us pray
   For Indonesia's prosperity:
   May her soil be fertile
   And spirited her soul,
   The nation and all the people.
   Conscious be her heart
   And her mind
   For Indonesia the Great.

   CHORUS

3. Indonesia, a sacred country,
   Our victorious country:
   There we stand
   Guarding our true Mother.
   Indonesia, a beaming Country,
   A country we love with all our heart,
   Let's make a vow
   That Indonesia be there forever.
   Blessed be her people
   And her sons,
   All her islands, and her seas.
   Fast be the country's progress
   And the progress of her youth
   For Indonesia the Great.

   CHORUS

IRAN

Author unknown

Music by
HASSAN RIAHI (b. 1945)
Arr. by W. L. REED

Chosen as a result of a competition held in 1990.

Sar Zad Az Ufuq Mihr-i Ḫāwarān
Furūg-i Dīda-yi Ḥaqq-bāwarān
Bahman - Farr-i Īman-i Māst
Payāmat Ay Imām Istiqlāl. Azādī-naqš-i Ğan-i Māst
Sahīdān - Pīčīda Dar Gūš-i Zamān Faryād-i Tān
Pāyanda Mānī Wa Ğawidān
Ğumhūrī-yi Islāmī-i Irān

Translation by W. L. Reed (from the German)

Upwards on the horizon rises the Eastern Sun,
The sight of the true Religion.
Bahman - the brilliance of our Faith.
Your message, O Imam, of independence and freedom
    is imprinted on our souls.
O Martyrs! The time of your cries of pain rings in our ears.
Enduring, continuing, eternal,
The Islamic Republic of Iran.

IRAQ

Words by
SHAFIQ ABDUL JABAR AL-KAMALI (1930 - 1984)

Music by
WALID GEORGES GHOLMIEH (b. 1938)
Arr. by W. L. REED

Adopted in 1981. This is the abridged, vocal version. There are seven verses in all, as well as instrumental sections in the full version of this National Anthem. Some of the other verses are given here.

2. *Hathihil-ardu Lehibun Wa Sana*
   Wa Shumukhum La Tudanini Sama
   Jabalun Yesmu Ala Hamil-duna
   Wa Suhulun Jassadat Fina-l-iba
   Babilun Fina Wa Ashourun Lena
   Wa Bina-l-tarikhu Yakhdallu Dia
   Nahnu Fin-nasi Jamana Wahduna
   Ghadbat As-sayfi Wa Hilm Al-anbiya.

3. *Ya Saraya Al-bathi Ya Usde-l-arin*
   Ya Shumukh Al-izzi Wal-majd It-talid
   Izahafi Kal-hawli Lin-nasri-l-mubin
   Wab Athi Fi Ardina Ahda-r-rashid
   Nahnu Jeel-ul-bathli Fajru-l-kadihin
   Ya Rihab Al-majd Udna Min Jadid
   Ummatun Nabni Bi Azmin La Yalim
   Wa Shahidun Yaqatfi Khatwa Shahid.

4. *Shabuna-l-jabbar Zahwun Wuntilaq*
   Wa Qila Al-izzi Yebniba Al-rifag
   Dumta Lil-urbi Malathan Ya Iraq
   Wa Shumusan Tajalu-l-layla Sabaha.

Translation

1. A homeland that extended its wings over the horizon,
   And wore the glory of civilisation as a garment –
   Blessed be the land of the two rivers,
   A homeland of glorious determination and tolerance.

2. This homeland is made of flame and splendour
   And pride unequalled by the high heavens.
   It is a mountain that rises above the tops of the world
   And a plain that embodies our pride.
   Babylon is inherent in us and Assyria is ours,
   And because of the glory of our background
   History itself radiates with light,
   And it is we alone who possess the anger of the sword
   And the patience of the prophets.

3. Oh company of al-Ba'th, you pride of lions,
   Oh pinnacle of pride and of inherited glory,
   Advance, bringing terror, to a certain victory
   And resurrect the time of al-Rashid in our land!
   We are a generation who give all and toil to the utmost.

4. Oh expanse of glory, we have returned anew
   To a nation that we build with unyielding determination.
   And each martyr follows in the footsteps of a former martyr.
   Our mighty nation is filled with pride and vigour
   And the comrades build the fortresses of glory.
   Oh Iraq, may you remain for ever a refuge for all the Arabs
   And be as suns that turn night into day!

IRISH REPUBLIC
Amhrán na bhFiann
(The Soldier's Song)

Words by
PEADAR KEARNEY (1883 - 1942)

Music by
PATRICK HEENEY (1881 - 1911)
Arr. by T. M. CARTLEDGE

Tempo di marcia

Sin - ne Fian - na Fáil, a - tá faoi gheall ag Éi - rinn,
Sol - diers are we, whose lives are pledged to Ire - land;

Buíon dár slua thar - toinn do rái - nig chughainn,
Some have come from a land be - yond the wave,

Faoi___ mhóid bheith saor, Sean - tir ár sin - sear
Sworn___ to be free, no more our an - cient

There were originally three verses and a chorus. The latter was adopted as the National Anthem in July 1926.

feas - ta Ní fhág - far faoin tior - án ná faoin
sire - land Shall shel - ter the des - pot or the

tráill. A - nocht a thé - am sa— bhear - na baoil, Le
slave. To - night we man— the— bear - na baoil,* In

gean ar Ghacil chun báis nó saoil, Le gun - na - scréach, faoi
Er - in's cause, come woe or weal, 'Mid can - non's— roar and

lámhach na— bpiléar, Seo libh can - aig amh - rán na bhFiann.
ri - fles— peal, We'll chant— a sol - dier's song.

* Pronounced 'Barna Bwail'. It means 'gap of danger'.

275

ISLE OF MAN

Words by
WILLIAM HENRY GILL (1839 - 1923)
Manx translation by
JOHN J. KNEEN (1873 - 1939)

Music adapted by
WILLIAM HENRY GILL (1839 - 1923)
From a Traditional Manx Air
Arr. by W. L. REED

Slow and stately

1. O___ land of our birth. O___ gem of God's
2. Then___ let us re - joice With___ heart, soul and
1. O___ Hal - loo nyn ghooie, O'___ Ch'lie - geen ny
2. Lhig___ dooin bog - goil bee, Lesh___ an - nym as

earth, O___ Is - land so strong and so
voice, And___ in The Lord's pro - mise con -
s'bwaaie Ry___ ghed - dyn er ooir aa - lin
cree, As___ cro - ghey er gial - dyn yn

There are eight verses in all. We give the first and last verses, which are those usually sung. W.H. Gill, a keen Manxman, was a collector and arranger of Manx music, of which he made a special study. J.J. Kneen was an expert on the Manx language and author of several books on it. For his scholarship he was awarded the Royal Norwegian Order of St. Olav by H.M. King Haakon VII in 1933, in recognition also of the historical connection between Norway and the Isle of Man.

fair;   Built___ firm   as   Bar - rool,
fide;   That___ each   sin - gle   hour
Yee,   Ta   dt'   Ard - stoyl   Reill - Thie
Chiarn;   Dy___ vod - mayd   dagh   oor,

Thy___   Throne   of   Home   Rule   Make   us
We___   trust   in   His   power,   No___
Myr___   Bar - rool   er   py hoie   Dy___
Treish___   teil   er   e   phooar,   Dagh___

free   as___   thy___   sweet   moun - tain   air.___
e - vil   our___   souls   can   be - tide.___
reayl   shin___   ayns___   seyr - snys   as   shee.___
olk   ass___   nyn___   an - mee - nyn   'hayrn.___

277

ISRAEL
Hatikvah
(The Hope)

Words by
NAFTALI HERZ IMBER (1856 - 1909)

Music by
NISSAN BELZER* or SAMUEL COHEN*
This is not certain.

Maestoso

Kol— od ba - le - vav pe - ni - mah Ne - fesh ye - hu - di
ho - mi - yah, Ul - fa - a - tei— miz - rach ka - di - mah A - yin le - zi - on
zo - fi - yah. Od lo av - dah tik - va - te - nu Ha - tik - vah bat

Adopted in 1948.
* Dates of birth and death unknown.

Translation

While yet within the heart - inwardly
The soul of the Jew yearns,
And towards the vistas of the East-eastwards
An eye to Zion looks.
'Tis not yet lost, our hope,
The hope of two thousand years,
To be a free people in our land
In the land of Zion and Jerusalem. } (twice)

ITALY
Inno di Mameli
(Mameli Hymn)

Words by
GOFFREDO MAMELI (1827 - 1849)

Music by
MICHELE NOVARO (1822 - 1885)

Adopted on 2 June, 1946, on the establishment of the Republic. There are five verses in all.

tel - li d'I - ta - lia, l'I - ta - lia s'è

des - ta, Del - l'el - mo di Sci - pio s'è

cin - ta la tes - la. Do - v'è la vit -

cresc. *rall.* **f** *a tempo*

to - ria? Le por - ga la chio - ma, Chè schia - va di

cresc. *rall.* **f** *a tempo*

Ro - ma Id - di - o la____ cre - ò.

Allegro mosso

Fra - tel - li d'I - ta - lia, l'I - ta - lia s'è

des - ta, Dell 'el - mo di Sci - pio s'è cin - ta la tes - ta. Dov' - è la vit -

to - ria? Le por - ga la chio - ma, Chè schia - va di Ro - ma Id - dio la cre -

Translation

Italian Brothers,
Italy has awakened,
She has wreathed her head
With the helmet of Scipio.
Where is Victory?
She bows her head to you,
You, whom God created
As the slave of Rome.
    (Repeat)
Let us band together, ⎫
We are ready to die, ⎬ (twice)
Italy has called us. ⎭

IVORY COAST

L'Abidjanaise
(Song of Abidjan)

Words by
MATHIEU EKRA (*b.* 1917)
in collaboration with JOACHIM BONY
and PIERRE MARIE COTY (*b.* 1927)

Music by
PIERRE MICHEL PANGO (*b.* 1926)
and PIERRE MARIE COTY (*b.* 1927)
Arr. by HENRY COLEMAN

Tempo di marcia moderato

Sa - lut ô ter - re d'es - pé - ran - ce;
Tes fils chè - re Côte d'I - voi - re

Pa - ys de l'hos - pi - ta - li - té. Tes lé - gions rem - plies de vail -
Fiers ar - ti - sans de ta gran - deur, Tous ras - sem - blés et pour ta

1.
lan - ce Ont re - le - vé ta di - gni - té.
gloi - re Te bâ - ti - ront dans le bon -

Adopted at the declaration of independence on 7 August, 1960.

284

à l'hu - ma - ni - té, En for - geant, u - nie dans la

foi nou - vel - le, La pa - trie de la vraie fra - ter - ni - té.

Translation by Elizabeth P. Coleman

We salute you, O land of hope,
Country of hospitality;
Thy gallant legions
Have restored thy dignity.
Beloved Ivory Coast, thy sons,
Proud builders of thy greatness,
All mustered together for thy glory,
In joy will construct thee.
Proud citizens of the Ivory Coast, the country calls us.
If we have brought back liberty peacefully,
It will be our duty to be an example
Of the hope promised to humanity,
Forging unitedly in new faith
The Fatherland of true brotherhood.

JAMAICA

Words by
HUGH BRAHAM SHERLOCK (*b.* 1905)*

Music by
ROBERT CHARLES LIGHTBOURNE (1909 - 1995)*
Arr. by MAPLETOFT POULLE *

1. E - ter-nal Fa - ther, bless our land, Guard us with Thy Migh - ty Hand, Keep us free from e - vil powers, Be our light through count - less hours. To our Lead - ers, Great De - fen - der,

Officially selected by the House of Representatives on 19 July, 1962.
* Mapletoft Poulle (1923 - 1981) blended the music (submitted separately to the National Anthem Committee) with the words (also submitted separately) to create the National Anthem.

2. Teach us true respect for all,
   Stir response to duty's call,
   Strengthen us the weak to cherish,
   Give us vision lest we perish.
   Knowledge send us, Heavenly Father,
   Grant true wisdom from above.

   CHORUS

JAPAN

Author unknown *

Music by
HIROMORI HAYASHI (1831 - 1896)
Arr. by W. L. REED

Ki - mi - ga— yo— wa Chi - yo - ni— Ya - chi - yo - ni Sa - za - ré -
i - shi no, I - wa - o to na - ri - té, Ko - ké no mu - su— ma - dé

Translation by Sazuko Takada

May thy peaceful reign last long!
May it last for thousands of years,
Until this tiny stone will grow into a massive rock
And the moss will cover it all deep and thick.

* Words selected from the seventh volume of *Kokinshu* dating from the 9th century.
First performed on 3 November, 1880, on Emperor Meiji's birthday, and approved on 12 August, 1893.

JORDAN

Words by
ABDUL-MONE'M AL-RIFAI' (1917 - 1985)

Music by
ABDUL-QADER AL-TANEER (1901 - 1957)

Translation

Long live the King!
Long live the King!
His position is sublime,
His banners waving in glory supreme.

Adopted on 25 May, 1946.

KAZAKHSTAN

Words by
MUZAFAR ALIMBAEV (*b.* 1923)

Music by
MUKAN TULEBAYEV (1913 - 1960)
and YEVGENY BRUSILOVSKY (1905 - 1981)
Arr. by W. L. REED

1. *Azatyk zholinda zhalyndap zhanypyz*
   Tagdyrdin tezinen, tozaktyn ozinen
   Aman-sau kalyppyz, aman-sau kalyppyz.

   CHORUS
   Erkindik kyrany, sharykta
   Eldikke shakyryp tirlikte!
   Alyptyn kuaty - khalykta,
   Khalyktyn kuaty - birlikte!

2. *Ardaktan anasyn, kyrmetten danasyn,*
   Bauyrga baskanbyz barshanyn balasyn.
   Tatulyk dostyktyn kieli besigi!
   Meyirban Uly Otan, Kazakhtyn dalasy!

   CHORUS

3. *Talaydy otkerdin, otkenge salauat,*
   Keleshek gazhayyp keleshek galamat!
   Ar-ozhdan, ana til onege-saltymyz,
   Erlik te, eldik te urlakka amanat!

   CHORUS

Translation

1. We are brave people, children of honesty.
   We sacrificed all on the way to liberty.
   We have survived the kicks of fortune,
   Hell's fire, and came off unhurt.

   CHORUS
   Fly high the eagle of freedom,
   Calling for unity!
   People have the power of the hero,
   And the power of people is in unity.

2. Respecting mothers and the genius of the people,
   In the evil times we were open to everybody.
   Kazakh steppe is our motherland,
   The holy cradle of friendship and solidarity.

   CHORUS

3. Let the past teach us a lesson,
   We believe in a bright future.
   We respect honour, dignity and our mother tongue.
   We pass on our traditions, courage
   And our state to future generations.

   CHORUS

KENYA

Words written collectively

Composer unknown

1. Ee Mu-ngu ngu-vu ye-tu I-le-te ba-ra-ka kwe-tu Ha-ki i-we nga-o na mli-nzi Na-tu-ka-e na u-du-gu A-ma-ni na u-hu-ru

1. O God of all cre-a-tion, Bless this— our land and na-tion. Just-ice be our shield and de-fend-er, May we dwell in un-i-ty, Peace and lib-er-ty.

Adopted on 12 December, 1963. Based on a traditional Kenya Folk Song which was adapted and harmonised by a National Commission of Five Musicians, who also wrote the words.

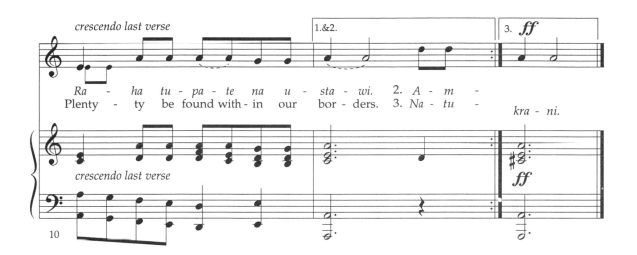

2. *Amkeni ndugu zetu*
   Tufanye sote bidii
   Nasi tujitoe kwa nguvu
   Nchiyetu ya Kenya tunayoipenda
   Tuwe tayari kuilinda.

3. *Natujenge taifa letu*
   Ee ndio wajibu wetu
   Kenya istahili heshima
   Tuungane mikono pamoja kazini
   Kila siku tuwe nashukrani.

2. Let one and all arise
   With hearts both strong and true.
   Service be our earnest endeavour,
   And our Homeland of Kenya,
   Heritage of splendour,
   Firm may we stand to defend.

3. Let all with one accord
   In common bond united,
   Build this our nation together,
   And the glory of Kenya,
   The fruit of our labour
   Fill every heart with thanksgiving.

KIRIBATI

Words and music by
URIUM TAMUERA IOTEBA (1910 - 1988)
Arr. by W. L. REED

First sung when independence was achieved on 12 July, 1979.

Ta - ua - ni - nne n te— ra - oi - roi, Ta - ngi - ri - a ao - ma - ta.

13

2. *Reken te kabaia ma te rau*
   Ibuakoia kaain abara
   Bon reken te nano ae banin
   Ma te i-tangitangiri naba.
   Ma ni wakina te kab'aia,
   Ma n neboa i eta abara.
   Ma ni wakina te kab'aia,
   Ma n neboa abara.

3. *Ti butiko ngkoe Atuara*
   Kawakinira ao kairira
   Nakon taai aika i maira.
   Buokira ni baim ae akoi.
   Kakabaia ara Tautaeka
   Ma ake a makuri iai.
   Kakabaia ara Tautaeka
   Ma aomata ni bane.

Translation

1. Stand up, Gilbertese!
   Sing with jubilation!
   Prepare to accept responsibility
   And to help each other!
   Be steadfastly righteous!
   Love all our people!
   Be steadfastly righteous!
   Love all our people!

2. The attainment of contentment
   And peace by our people
   Will be achieved when all
   Our hearts beat as one,
   Love one another!
   Promote happiness and unity!
   Love one another!
   Promote happiness and unity!

3. We beseech You, O God,
   To protect and lead us
   In the days to come.
   Help us with Your loving hand.
   Bless our Government
   And all our people!
   Bless our Government
   And all our people!

KOREA (NORTH)

Words by
PAK SE YONG (1902 - 1989)

Music by
KIM WON GYUN (*b.* 1917)
Arr. by W. L. REED

Fairly slowly and solemnly

1. A ch'im ŭn pin na-ra i kang - san Ŭn -

gum e, cha - wŏn do ka - dŭk han Sam - ch'ol - li, a - rŭm-da - un

nae cho - guk, Pan - man - nyŏn ora - en ryŏk - sa e. Ch'al -

Adopted in 1947.

298

2. *Paektusan kisang ŭl ta anko.*
   Kŭllo ŭi chŏngsin ŭn kittŭrŏ.
   Chilli ro mungch 'yŏ jin ŏksen ttŭt
   On segye apsŏ nagari.
   Sonnŭn him nodo do naemirŏ,
   Inmin ŭi ttŭs ŭro sŏn nara.
   Han ŏpsi pugang hanŭn
   I chosŏn kiri pinnaese.

Translation

1. Let morning shine on the silver and gold of this land,
   Three thousand leagues packed with natural wealth.
   My beautiful fatherland.
   The glory of a wise people
   Brought up in a culture brilliant
   With a history five millennia long.
   Let us devote our bodies and minds
   To supporting this Korea for ever.

2. The firm will, bonded with truth,
   Nest for the spirit of labour,
   Embracing the atmosphere of Mount Paektu,
   Will go forth to all the world.
   The country established by the will of the people,
   Breasting the raging waves with soaring strength.
   Let us glorify for ever this Korea,
   Limitlessly rich and strong.

KOREA (SOUTH)

Words by
YUN CH'I-HO (1865 - 1946)
or AN CH'ANG-HO (1878 - 1938)

Music by
AHN EAKTAY (1905 - 1965)

1. Tong - hai mool - kwa paik - tu - san - i Ma - ru - go tal - to - rok
Ha - na - nim - i po - ho - ha - sa U - ri na - ra man - sei.

Officially adopted on 15 August, 1948.

2. *Namsan uye chusonamu*
   Chulkapeul turultut.
   Paramisul pulbyunhamum
   Uri kisang ilsae.

   CHORUS

English versification by Whami Koh and T. M. Cartledge

1. Tong-Hai Sea and Pakdoo Mountain, so long as they endure,
   May God bless Korea our land for endless ages to come!

   CHORUS
   North to south bedecked with flowers, land of beauty rare,
   May God keep our country united and preserve our land.

2. Eternally Naamsaan's pine-trees stand like an armour sure,
   Through whatever tempest or danger, as our symbol of strength.

   CHORUS

302

KUWAIT

Words by
AHMAD MUSHARI AL-ADWANI (1923 - 1992)

Music by
IBRAHIM NASIR AL-SOULA (*b.* 1935)
Arr. by W. L. REED

Adopted in 1978.

1. *Watanil Kuwait Salemta Lilmajdi*
   Wa Ala Jabeenoka Tali-Ossaadi
   Watanil Kuwait
   Watanil Kuwait
   Watanil Kuwait Salemta Lilmajdi.

2. *Ya Mahda Abaa-il Ola Katabou*
   Sefral Khloudi Fanadati Shohobo
   Allaho Akbar Ehnahom Arabo
   Talaat Kawakebo Jannatil Kholdi
   Watanil Kuwait Salemta Lilmajdi.

3. *Bourekta Ya Watanil Kuwaita Lana*
   Sakanan Wa Eshta Alal Mada Watana
   Yafdeeka Horron Fi Hemaka Bana
   Sarhol Hayati Be Akramil Aydi
   Watanil Kuwait Salemta Lilmajdi.

4. *Nahmeeka Ya Watani Wa Shahidona*
   Sharoul Hoda Wal Haqqo Ra-Edona
   Wa Amirona Lil Ezzi Qa-Edona
   Rabbol Hamiyati Sadqol Waadi
   Watanil Kuwait Salemta Lilmajdi.

Translation

1. Kuwait, Kuwait, Kuwait,
   My country,
   In peace live, in dignity,
   Your face bright,
   Your face bright,
   Your face bright with majesty,
   Kuwait, Kuwait Kuwait,
   My country.

2. Oh cradle of ancestry,
   Who put down its memory
   With everlasting symmetry,
   Showing all eternity,
   Those Arabs were Heavenly,
   Kuwait, Kuwait, Kuwait,
   My country.

3. Blessed be
   My country,
   A homeland for harmony,
   Warded by true sentry,
   Giving their souls aptly,
   Building high its history,
   Kuwait, Kuwait Kuwait,
   My country.

4. We're for you, My country,
   Led by faith and loyalty,
   With its Prince equally,
   Fencing us all fairly,
   With warm love and verity,
   Kuwait, Kuwait Kuwait,
   My country,
   In peace live, in dignity.

KYRGYZSTAN

Words by
ZH. SADIKOVA
and SH. KULUEVA*

Music by
N. DAVLYESOVA
and K. MOLDOVASANOVA*
Arr. by W. L. REED

Adopted on 18 December, 1992.
* Dates of birth unknown.

1.	*Vysokie gory, doliny, polia,*
	Rodnaia, zavetnaia nasha zemlia,
	Otsy nashi zhili sredi Ala-Too
	Vsegda svoiu rodinu sviato khrania.

	CHORUS
	Vpered, kyrgzskii narod,
	Putem svobody vpered
	Vzrastai, narod, rastsvetai,
	Svoiu sud'bu sozidai.

2.	*Izvechno narod nash dlia druzby otkryt*
	Edinstvo i druzhbu on v serdtse khranit
	Zemlia Kyrgyzstana rodnaia strana
	Luchami soglasia ozarena.

	CHORUS

3.	*Mechty i nadezhdy naroda sbylis'*
	I znamia svobody voznositsia vvys'.
	Nasled'e otsov nashikh peredadim
	Na blago naroda potomkam svoim.

	CHORUS

Translation

1.	High mountains, valleys and fields
	Are our native, holy land.
	Our fathers lived amidst the Ala-Toe,
	Always saving their motherland.

	CHORUS
	Come on, Kyrgyz people,
	Come on to freedom!
	Stand up and flourish!
	Create your fortune!

2.	We are open for freedom for ages.
	Friendship and unity are in our hearts.
	The land of Kyrgyzstan, our native state,
	Shining in the rays of consent.

	CHORUS

3.	Dreams of the people came true,
	And the flag of liberty is over us.
	The heritage of our fathers we will
	Pass to our sons for the benefit of people.

	CHORUS

LAOS

Words by
SISANA SISANE (*b.* 1922)

Music by
THONGDY SOUNTHONEVICHIT (1905 - 1968)

Xat - lao tang-tae day - ma lao thook-thua - na xeut-xoo soo-

tchay, Huam - haeng huam-chit huam - chay sa-mak-khi-kan pen kam-lang di-

ao. Det - diao phom-kan kao - na boo - xa xü-kiat khong

Adopted in 1947. New text adopted in 1975.

Translation

For all time the Lao people have glorified their Fatherland,
United in heart, spirit and vigour as one.
Resolutely moving forwards,
Respecting and increasing the dignity of the Lao people
And proclaiming the right to be their own masters.
The Lao people of all origins are equal
And will no longer allow imperialists and traitors to harm them.
The entire people will safeguard the independence
And the freedom of the Lao nation.
They are resolved to struggle for victory
In order to lead the nation to prosperity.

LATVIA

Words and music by
KARLIS BAUMANIS (1834 - 1904)

Originally written as an entry for a singing festival in 1873, it very soon became the National Anthem.

dē - li dzied, Laid mums tur lat - mē diet, Mūs
Lat - vi - ja. Lat - vi - ja.

Versification by George A. Simons

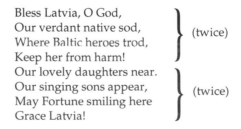

Bless Latvia, O God,
Our verdant native sod,   } (twice)
Where Baltic heroes trod,
Keep her from harm!
Our lovely daughters near.
Our singing sons appear,   } (twice)
May Fortune smiling here
Grace Latvia!

LEBANON

Words by
RACHID NAKHLÉ (1873 - 1939)

Music by
WADIH SABRA (1876 - 1952)

Adopted officially by Presidential decree on 12 July, 1927.

2. *Chaykhouna Oualfata Indasaôutil Oua Tann*
   Ousdou ghâ Bin Mata Saouarat Nalfitann
   Charkouna Kalbouhou Aba Dann Loubnane
   Sanahou Rab Bouhou Limadal Azmane.
   Koullouna Lilouatann Lil' Oula Lil 'Alam,
   Koullouna Lilouatann.

3. *Bahrouhou Barrouhou Dourratouchchar Kain*
   Rildouhou Birrouhou Malioul Koutbaïn
   Ismouhou 'Izzouhou Moun Zou Kânal Joudoude
   Majdouhu Arzouhou Ramzouhou Lilkhouloude
   Koullouna Lilouatann Lil' Oula Lil 'Alam,
   Koullouna Lilouatann.

Translation

1. All of us! For our Country, for our Flag and Glory!
   Our valour and our writings are the envy of the ages.
   Our mountains and our valleys, they bring forth stalwart men.
   And to Perfection all our efforts we devote.
   All of us! For our Country, for our Flag and Glory!

2. Our Elders and our children, they await our Country's call:
   And on the Day of Crisis they are as Lions of the Jungle.
   The heart of our East is ever Lebanon:
   May God preserve her until end of time.
   All of us! For our Country, for our Flag and Glory!

3. The Gems of the East are her land and sea.
   Throughout the world her good deeds flow from pole to pole.
   And her name is her glory since time began.
   Immortality's Symbol- the Cedar- is her Pride.
   All of us! For our Country, for our Flag and Glory!

LESOTHO

Words by
FRANÇOIS COILLARD (1834 - 1904)

Music by
FERDINAND-SAMUEL LAUR (1791 - 1854)

1. Le - so - tho fa - t͡se la bo - nta - t'a ro - na, Ha - r'a ma - fa -
t͡se le le - tle ke lo - na. Ke moo re hla - hi - leng,
Ke moo re ho - li - leng, Re - a le ra - ta.

The Government adopted this as their National Anthem on 2 May, 1967, using the first and last verses of the words written by a French missionary.

2. *Molimo ak'u boloke Lesotho,*
   U felise lintoa le matŝoenyeho.
   Oho fatŝe lena,
   La bo-ntat'a rona,
   Le be le khotso.

Translation

1. Lesotho, land of our Fathers,
   You are the most beautiful country of all.
   You give us birth,
   In you we are reared
   And you are dear to us.

2. Lord, we ask You to protect Lesotho.
   Keep us free from conflict and tribulations.
   Oh, land of mine,
   Land of our Fathers,
   May you have peace.

LIBERIA

Words by
DANIEL BASHIEL WARNER (1815 - 1880)*

Music by
OLMSTEAD LUCA (*b.* 1836)†

1. All hail, Li-be-ria, hail! All hail, Li-be-ria, hail! This glo-rious land of li-ber-ty Shall long be ours.____ Though new her name, Green be her fame, And migh-ty be her

Adopted on 26 July, 1847.
* Third President of Liberia, 1864 - 1868.
† Year of birth uncertain and year of death unknown.

2. All hail, Liberia, hail!
   All hail, Liberia, hail!
   In union strong success is sure.
   We cannot fail!
   With God above
   Our rights to prove,
   We will o'er all prevail! } (twice)

   With heart and hand our country's cause defending,
   We'll meet the foe with valour unpretending.
   Long live Liberia, happy land!
   A home of glorious liberty }
   By God's command! } (twice)

322

LIBYA
(Libyan Arab Jamahiriya)

Words by
ABDALLA SHAMS EL-DIN (1921 - 1977)

Music by
MAHMOUD EL-SHERIF (1912 - 1990)
Arr. by W. L. REED

Al - la - hu Ak - bar___ Al - la - hu Ak - bar___ Al - la - hu

Adopted on 1 September, 1969, when Libya became a republic.

Ya Hadihi Ddunya Atilli Wa 'Smai
Gaisu L-aadi Ga'a Yabgi Masrai
Bil-haqqi Saufa Fa-saufa Afnihi Mai.

Qulu Mai L-wailu Lil-mustamiri
Wa Llahu Fauqa L-gadiri L-mutagabbiri
Allahu Akbaru Ya Biladi Kabbiri
Wa-hudi Binasiyati L-mugiri Wa-dammiri.

God is greatest!
God is greatest!
He is above the plots of the aggressors,
And He is the best helper of the oppressed.
With faith and with weapons I shall defend my country,
And the light of truth will shine in my hand.
Sing with me!
Sing with me!
God is greatest!
God is greatest!
God, God, God is greatest!
God is above the aggressors.

O World, look up and listen!
The enemy's army is coming,
Wishing to destroy me.
With truth and with my gun I shall repulse him.

And should I be killed,
I would kill him with me.
Sing with me -
Woe to the Imperialists!
And God is above the treacherous tyrant.
God is greatest!
Therefore glorify Him, O my country,
And seize the forehead of the tyrant
And destroy him!

LIECHTENSTEIN

Words by
JAKOB JOSEPH JAUCH (1802 - 1859)

Composer unknown

1. O - ben am jun - gen Rhein Leh - net sich Liech - ten - stein An Al - pen - höh'n. Dies lie - be Hei - mat - land, Das teu - re Va - ter - land, Hat Got - tes— wei - ser Hand Für— uns er - seh'n.

The original five verses were written in 1850. The words were slightly changed in 1963, and only the first and last verses are currently used. The melody is the same as that of the National Anthem of the United Kingdom.

2. *Hoch lebe Liechtenstein,*
   Blühend am jungen Rhein,
   Glücklich und treu.
   Hoch leb'der Fürst vom Land,
   Hoch unser Vaterland, } (twice)
   Durch Bruderliebe-Band
   Vereint und frei.

Translation

1. High above the young Rhine
   Lies Liechtenstein, resting
   On Alpine heights.
   This beloved homeland,
   This dear fatherland } (twice)
   Was chosen for us by
   God's wise hand.

2. Long live Liechtenstein,
   Blossoming on the young Rhine,
   Happy and faithful!
   Long live the Prince of the Land,
   Long live our fatherland, } (twice)
   United by brotherly bonds and free!

LITHUANIA

Words and music by
VINCAS KUDIRKA (1858 - 1899)

First appeared in print in 1896.
Became the National Anthem in 1918.

Tam - su - mus pra - 'sa - li - na   Ir 'svie - sa   ir tie - sa
De - ga mū - sų   'sir - dy - se   Var - dan tos   Lie - tu - vos

Mūs 'zings - nius te - ly - di—   Vie - ny - bė te - 'zy - di!

Versification

1. Lithuania, land of heroes,
   Thou our Fatherland that art,
   From the glorious deeds of ages
   Shall Thy children take heart.
   May Thy children ever follow
   Their heroic fathers
   In devotion to their country
   And good will to others.

2. May the sun of our loved shore
   Shine upon us evermore;
   May the right and the truth
   Keep our pathway lighted.
   May the love of our dear land
   Make us strong of heart and hand,
   May our land ever stand
   Peaceful and united.

LUXEMBOURG
Ons Hémécht
(Our Motherland)

Words by
MICHEL LENTZ (1820 - 1893)

Music by
JEAN-ANTOINE ZINNEN (1827 - 1898)
Arr. by MARTIN SHAW

First performed on 5 June, 1864, this became the National Anthem in 1895. There are four verses in all.

as   onst Land, fir   dat   mir   géif,   Hei - ni - dden   al - les

won.   Onst   Hee - mechts - land,   dat   mir   sou déif   An

on - sen Hier - zer   dron._____   Onst   Hee - mechts - land,   dat

mir   sou déit   An   on - sen Hier - zer   dron._____

2. *O Du do uewen, deem séng Hand*
   Duurch d'Welt d'Natioune leet,
   Behitt Du d'Lëtzebuerger Land
   Vru friemem Joch a Leed!
   Du hues ons all als Kanner schon
   De fräie Geescht jo gin.
   Looss viru blénken d'Fräiheetssonn,
   Déi mir sou laang gesin.

Translation by Fabio Lazzati

1. Where the Alzette flows through the meadows,
   The Sura breaks through the crags.
   Where the vine fragrant grows along the Moselle,
   The sky promises us wine:
   There lies the land for which we willingly
   Dare everything down here.
   Our Homeland which we so deeply
   Carry in our hearts.

2. O Thou above, Whose powerful hand
   Leads athe nations through the world,
   Protect the Luxembourg land
   From foreign yoke and threat.
   As children Thou already instilled in us all
   The spirit of freedom.
   Let freedom's sun, which we have known for so long,
   Shine for evermore.

French version

1. *Où l'Alzette arrose champs et prés,*
   La Sûre baigne les rochers;
   Où la Moselle, riante et belle,
   Nous fait cadeau du vin,
   C'est notre pays pour lequel
   Nous risquons tout sur terre;
   Notr' chère et adorable partie
   Dont notr' âme est remplie.

2. *O Toi aux cieux qui nuit et jour*
   Diriges les nations du monde;
   Écarte du pays de Luxembourg
   L'oppression étrangère
   Enfants nous avons reçu de Toi
   L'esprit de la liberté.
   Permets au soleil de liberté
   De luire à tout jamais.

Translation by Fabio Lazzati

1. Where the Alzette waters fields and meadows,
   The Sura washes the crags;
   Where the Moselle, smiling and beautiful,
   Presents us with wine:
   That is our land for which
   We dare everything down here;
   Our dear and adorable Motherland,
   With which our heart is filled.

2. O Thou in heaven, Who night and day
   Leadest the nations of the world;
   Avert from the land of Luxembourg
   The foreign yoke.
   As children we received from You
   The spirit of freedom.
   Let freedom's sun
   Shine for evermore.

MACEDONIA

Words by
VLADO MALESKI (1919 - 1984)

Music by
TODOR SKALOVSKI (*b.* 1909)
Arr. by W. L. REED

With dignity (♩ = 88)

1. De - nes nad Ma - ke - do - ni - ja se ra - gja

No - vo son - ce - na slo - bo - da - ta, Ma - ke -

don - ci - te se bo - rat Za svoj - te prav - di -

Officially adopted on 11 August, 1992.

ni,_____ Ma - ke - don - ci - te se bo - rat_____ Za_____

svoj - te prav - di - ni._____ 2. Od - zi - ve - e._____

2. *Odnovo sega znameto se vee*
   Na Krusevskata Republika
   Goce Delcev, Pitu Guli,
   Dame Gruev, Sandanski. } *(twice)*

3. *Gorite Makedonski sumno peat*
   Novi pesni, novi vesnici,
   Makedonija slobodna
   Slobodna zivee. } *(twice)*

Translation by T. Dragadze

1. Today over Macedonia
   A new sun of freedom rises,
   Macedonians fight
   For their rights. } (twice)

2. Now once again flies
   The flag of the Krusevo Republic,
   Goce Delcev, Pitu Guli,
   Dame Gruev, Sandanski. } (twice)

3. The Macedonian woodlands sing brightly
   New songs, new awakenings.
   Free Macedonia
   Lives free. } (twice)

MADAGASCAR

Words by
Pasteur RAHAJASON (1897 - 1971)

Music by
NORBERT RAHARISOA (*d.* 1964)*
Arr. by HENRY COLEMAN

Adopted on 21 October, 1958.
* Year of birth unknown.

2. *Ry Tanindrazanay malala ô*
   Irinay mba hanompoan'anao.
   Ny tena sy fo fanahy anananay 'zay sarobidy
   Sy mendrika tokoa.

   CHORUS

3. *Ry Tanindrazanay malala ô*
   Irinay mba hitahian' anao.
   Ka Ilay Nahary 'zao ton tolo izao no
   Fototra ijoroan, ny satanao.

   CHORUS

Translation

1. O, our beloved fatherland,
   O, fair Madagascar,
   Our love will never decay,
   But will last eternally.

   CHORUS
   O, Lord Creator, do Thou bless
   This Island of our Fathers,   } (twice)
   That she may be happy and prosperous
   For our own satisfaction.

2. O, our beloved fatherland,
   Let us be thy servant
   With body, heart and spirit
   In dear and worthy service.

   CHORUS

3. O, our beloved fatherland,
   May God bless thee,
   That created all lands;
   In order He maintains thee.

   CHORUS

MALAWI

Words* and music by
MICHAEL-FREDRICK PAUL SAUKA (*b.* 1934)

1. *Mlu - ngu da - li - tsa - ni Ma - la - wi,*
1. O God bless our land of Ma - la - wi,

Mum - su - nge m'mte - nde - re. Go - nje - tsa - ni
Keep it a land of peace. Put down each and

a - da - ni o - nse, Nja - la, nthe - nda, nsa - nje.
ev - 'ry e - ne - my, Hung - er, dis - ease, en - vy.

* The official text is given in Chichewa and English. The Chitumbuka version is no longer used.
Selected as a result of a competition held in February 1964, and first played publicly on Independence Day, 6 July, 1964.

2. *Malawi ndziko lokongola,*
   La chonde ndi ufulu,
   Nyanja ndi mphepo ya m'mapiri,
   Ndithudi tadala.
   Zigwa, mapiri, nthaka, dzinthu,
   N'mphatso zaulere.
   Nkhalango, madambo abwino.
   Ngwokoma Malawi.

3. *O Ufulu tigwirizane,*
   Kukweza Malawi.
   Ndi chikondi, khama, kumvera,
   Timutumikire.
   Pa nkhondo nkana pa mtendere,
   Cholinga n'chimodzi.
   Mai, bambo, tidzipereke,
   Pokweza Malawi.

Versification

2. Our own Malawi, this land so fair,
   Fertile and brave and free.
   With its lakes, refreshing mountain air,
   How greatly blest are we.
   Hills and valleys, soil so rich and rare
   Give us a bounty free.
   Wood and forest, plains so broad and fair,
   All - beauteous Malawi.

3. Freedom ever, let us all unite
   To build up Malawi.
   With our love, our zeal and loyalty,
   Bringing our best to her.
   In time of war, or in time of peace,
   One purpose and one goal.
   Men and women serving selflessly
   In building Malawi.

MALAYSIA

Words written collectively

Music by
PIERRE JEAN DE BERANGER (1780 - 1857)

Adopted when Malaya achieved independence on 31 August, 1957. It was previously known in Malaya and Indonesia as a popular song called Terang Bulan (Moonlight), but this popular version of the tune is now banned. When Malaysia was founded in 1963 this was retained as the National Anthem.
Malaysia also has thirteen State Anthems (see NATIONAL ANTHEMS OF THE WORLD – 5th Edition).

Translation

My country, my native land.
The people living united and progressive,
May God bestow blessing and happiness.
May our Ruler have a successful reign.
May God bestow blessing and happiness.
May our Ruler have a successful reign.

THE MALDIVES

Words by
MOHAMED JAMEEL DIDI (1915 - 1989)

Music by
WANNAKUWATTAWADUGE DON AMARADEVA (*b.* 1927)
Arr. by W. L. REED

The music was composed and adopted in 1972. There are eight verses. We print only those that are normally sung at public gatherings.

Translation

CHORUS
In National Unity do we salute our Nation.
In the National language do we offer our prayers
And salute our Nation.

1. We bow in respect to the Emblem of our Nation,
   And salute the Flag so exalted.

   CHORUS

2. We salute the colours of our Flag;
   Green, Red and White,
   Which symbolise Victory, Blessing and Success.

   CHORUS

MALI

Words by
SEYDOU BADIAN KOUYATÉ (*b.* 1928)

Music by
BANZOUMANA SISSOKO (1890 - 1987)
Arr. by HENRY COLEMAN

Adopted by the National Assembly on 9 August, 1962.

mi dé - couvre son front Au de - dans ou au de - hors De -

bout sur les rem - parts Nous som - mes ré - so - lus de mou - rir.

CHORUS

Pour l'A - frique et pour toi, Ma - li,
li d'au - jour - d'hui, O Ma - li, de de - main Les champs fleu

rall. 2nd time

No - tre dra - peau se - ra li - ber - té.
ris - sent d'es - pé - ran - ce, Les coeurs vi - brent de con-

rall. 2nd time

Pour l'A-frique et pour toi Ma-li No-tre com-bat

se - ra u - ni - té. O Ma - fian - ce.

2. Debout, villes et campagnes,
Debout, femmes, jeunes et vieux
Pour la Patrie en marche
Vers l'avenir radieux
Pour notre dignité.
Renforçons bien nos rangs,
Pour le salut public
Forgeons le bien commun
Ensemble, au coude à coude
Faisons le chantier du bonheur.

CHORUS

3. La voie est dure, très dure
Qui mène au bonheur commun.
Courage et dévouement
Vigilance à tout moment,
Courage et dévouement
Vigilance à tout moment,
Vérité des temps anciens,
Vérité de tous les jours,
Le bonheur par le labeur
Fera la Mali de demain.

CHORUS

4. L'Afrique se lève enfin
Saluons ce jour nouveau.
Saluons la liberté,
Marchons vers l'unité.
Dignité retrouvée
Soutient notre combat.
Fidelès à notre serment
De faire l'Afrique unie
Ensemble, debout mes frères
Tous au rendez-vous de l'honneur.

CHORUS

Translation by T. M. Cartledge

1. At your call, Mali,
   So that you may prosper,
   Faithful to your destiny,
   We shall all be united,
   One people, one goal, one faith
   For a united Africa.
   If the enemy should show himself
   Within or without,
   On the ramparts,
   We are ready to stand and die.

   CHORUS
   For Africa and for you, Mali,
   Our banner shall be liberty.
   For Africa and for you, Mali,
   Our fight shall be for unity.
   Oh, Mali of today,
   Oh, Mali of tomorrow,
   The fields are flowering with hope
   And hearts are thrilling with confidence.

2. Stand up, towns and countryside,
   Stand up, women, stand up young and old,
   For the Fatherland on the road
   Towards a radiant future.
   For the sake of our dignity
   Let us strengthen our ranks;
   For the public well-being
   Let us forge the common good.
   Together, shoulder to shoulder,
   Let us work for happiness.

   CHORUS

3. The road is hard, very hard,
   That leads to common happiness.
   Courage and devotion,
   Constant vigilance,
   Courage and devotion,
   Constant vigilance,
   Truth from olden times,
   The truths of every day,
   Happiness through effort
   Will build the Mali of tomorrow.

   CHORUS

4. Africa is at last arising,
   Let us greet this new day.
   Let us greet freedom,
   Let us march towards unity.
   Refound dignity
   Supports our struggle.
   Faithful to our oath
   To make a united Africa,
   Together, arise, my brothers,
   All to the place where honour calls.

   CHORUS

MALTA
Innu Malti
(Hymn of Malta)

Words by
DUN KARM PSAILA (1871 - 1961)

Music by
ROBERT SAMMUT (1870 - 1934)

Dun Karm Psaila was asked to write these words for a school hymn to Sammut's music. He conceived the idea of writing a hymn to Malta in the form of a prayer; he wanted to unite all parties with the strong ties of religion and love of country.

It was first performed on 3 February, 1923, and officially became the National Anthem in 1945.

lej,_____ kif dej - jem Int____ ħa - rist:_____
land_____ so dear whose name__ we__ bear!_____

Fta - kar li lil - ha bl - oħ - la dawl__ lib__ bist!_____
Keep her in mind____ whom Thou hast made__ so__ fair!_____

2. *Agħti, kbir Alla, iddeħen lil min jaħkimha,*
   Rodd ilħniena lissid ,saħħa 'lħaddiem:
   Seddaq ilgħaqda fil-Maltin u ssliem!

Translation by May Butcher

2. May he who rules for wisdom be regarded,
   In master mercy, strength in man increase!
   Confirm us all in unity and peace!

MARSHALL ISLANDS
Forever Marshall Islands

Words and music by
AMATA KABUA (*b.* 1928)
Arr. by W. L. REED

Slowly

Ae - lōñ eo aō ion lo - me - to;
My is - land lies o'er the ____ o - cean;

Ein - wot wut ko lōti ion dren ____ e - lae; Kin me - ram in
Like a wreath of flowers up - on ____ the sea; With the light of

Me - kar jen ijo ____ i - lañ; Err - eo an romak ioir kin me - ram
Me - kar from far ____ a - bove; Shin - ing with the bril - liance of rays

Il - tan pein A - nij ewel - eo_____ im woj; Ke - jolit kij kin
Our__ Fa - ther's won - drous cre - a - tion; Be - queathed to

ijin ji - kir_____ e - mol; Ij - ja - min i - lok jen in aō -
us our Mo - ther - land; I'll__ ne - ver leave my dear home

le - mo ran;_____ An - ij an ro je - mem wo - nak - ke
__ sweet home;_____ God of our fore - fa - thers pro - tect and

im kej - ram - mon Ae - liñ kein am.
bless for e - ver Mar - shall Is - lands.

MAURITANIA

No words

Music by
TOLIA NIKIPROWETZKY (*b.* 1916)

Based on traditional music, and adopted in 1960, the year of independence.

D. % al Fine

MAURITIUS

Words by
JEAN GEORGES PROSPER (*b.* 1933)

Music by
PHILIPPE GENTIL (*b.* 1928)

Glo - ry to thee, Mo - ther - land, O mo - ther - land of mine. Sweet is thy beau - ty, Sweet is thy fra - grance, A - round thee we ga - ther As

Selected by means of a competition, and came into use when the country attained independence on 12 March, 1968.

one peo-ple, As one na-tion, In peace, jus-tice___ and li-ber-

ty._____ Be - lov - ed coun-try, may

God___ bless___ thee For e - ver and e - ver.

MEXICO

Words by
FRANCISCO GONZÁLEZ BOCANEGRA (1824 - 1861)

Music by
JAIME NUNÓ (1824 - 1908)

Me - xi - ca - nos al gri - to - de gue - rra El a-
ce - ro a - pre-stad y el bri-dón,— Y re-
tiem - ble en sus cen - tros la tie - rra, Al so-

Adopted on 16 September, 1854. There are four verses.

no - ro ru-gir del— ca - ñón, Y re-

tiem - ble en sus cen - tros la tie - rra, Al so-

FINE

no - ro ru-gir del— ca - ñón.

FINE

p **VERSE**

1. Ci - ña ¡oh Pa - tria! tus sie - nes de o - li - va De la

p

paz____ el ar - cán - gel di - vi - no, Que en el

cie - lo tu e - ter - no des - ti - no Por el

de - do de Dios se es - cri - bió. Mas si o-

sa - re un ex - tra - ño e - ne - mi - go Pro - fa-

nar —— con su plan - ta tu sue - lo, Pien - sa ¡oh

Pa - tria que - ri - da! que el cie - lo Un sol-

da - do en ca - da hi - jo te dió, Un —— sol -

D.C. al Fine

da - do en ca - da hi - jo te dió.

D.C. al Fine

ff

2. *¡Patria! ¡Patria! Tus hijos te juran*
   Exhalar en tus aras su aliento,
   Si el clarín, con su bélico acento,
   Los convoca a lidiar con valor.
   ¡Para ti las guirnaldas de oliva!
   ¡Un recuerdo para ellos de gloria!
   ¡Un laurel para ti de victoria!
   ¡Un sepulcro para ellos de honor!   *(twice)*

CHORUS

Translation by T. M. Cartledge

CHORUS
Mexicans, when the war cry is heard,
Have sword and bridle ready.
Let the earth's foundations tremble } (twice)
At the loud cannon's roar.

1. May the divine archangel crown your brow,
   Oh fatherland, with an olive branch of peace,
   For your eternal destiny has been written
   In heaven by the finger of God.
   But should a foreign enemy
   Dare to profane your soil with his tread,
   Know, beloved fatherland, that heaven gave you
   A soldier in each of your sons.   (twice)

CHORUS

2. Fatherland, oh fatherland, your sons vow
   To give their last breath on your altars,
   If the trumpet with its warlike sound
   Calls them to valiant battle.
   For you, the garlands of olive,
   For them, a glorious memory.
   For you, the victory laurels,
   For them, an honoured tomb.   (twice)

CHORUS

MICRONESIA

Arr. by
W. L. REED

1. We peo-ple of Mi-cro-ne-sia Ex-er-cise sov-'reign-ty.
Es-tab-lish our Con sti-tu-tion Of Fe-de-ra-ted States.___
Af-firm our com-mon wish to live In peace and har-mo-ny.

Details of author and composer not yet available.

CHORUS

To pre-serve he-ri-tage of past And pro-mise of fu-ture.—

f Make one na-tion— Of ma-ny isles,— Di-ver-si-

ty— Of our cul-tures.— Our diff'-ren-ces— Will en-rich

us,— Wa-ters bring us— All to-ge-ther.— They don't sep'-

2. Our Ancestors made their homes here,
   Displaced no other man,
   We who remain wish unity,
   Been ruled we seek freedom,
   Our days began when men explored
   Seas in rafts and canoes.
   Our nation born when men voyaged
   The seas via the stars.

   CHORUS

3. The world itself is an island
   We seen from all nations.
   Peace, friendship, co-operation,
       love and humanity.
   With this Constitution,
       we now become proud guardian
   Of our beautiful islands.

   CHORUS

MOLDOVA

Limba Noastră
(Our Tongue)

Words by
ALEXEI MATEEVICI *

Music by
ALEXANDRU CRISTI *
Arr. by W. L. REED

Officially adopted on 7 June, 1994.

* Dates of author and composer not yet available.

1. Limba noastră-i o comoară
   În adîncuri înfundată,
   Un şirag de piatră rară
   Pe moşie revărsată.
   Limba noastră-i foc ce arde
   Într-un neam, ce fără veste
   S-a trezit din somn de moarte
   Ca viteazul din poveste.
   Limba noastră-i numai cîntec,
   Doina dorurilor noastre,
   Roi de fulgere, ce spintec
   Nouri negri, zări albastre.

2. Limba noastră-i graiul pîinii,
   Cînd de vînt se mişcă vara;
   În rostirea ei bătrînii
   Cu sudori sfinţit-au ţara.
   Limba noastră-i frunză verde,
   Zbuciumul din codrii veşnici,
   Nistrul lin, ce-n valuri pierde
   Ai luceferilor sfeşnici.
   Nu veţi plînge-atunci amarnic,
   Că vi-i limba prea săracă,
   Si-ţi vedea, cît îi de darnic
   Graiul ţării noastre dragă.

3. Limba noastră-i vechi izvoade.
   Povestiri din alte vremuri;
   Şi citindu-le 'nşirate,
   Te-nfiori adînc şi tremuri.
   Limba noastră îi aleasă
   Să ridice slavă-n ceruri,
   Să ne spiue-n hram şi-acasă
   Veşnicele adevăruri.
   Limba noastră-i limba sfîntă,
   Limba vechilor cazanii,
   Care o plîng şi care o cîntă
   Pe la vatra lor ţăranii.

4. Înviaţi-vă dar graiul,
   Ruginit de multă vreme,
   Ştergeţi slinul, mucegaiul
   Al uitării 'n care geme.
   Strîngeţi piatra lucitoare
   Ce din soare se aprinde –
   Şi-ţi avea în revărsare
   Un potop nou de cuvinte.
   Răsări-va o comoară
   În adîncuri înfundată,
   Un şirag de piatră rară
   Pe moşie revărsată.

Translation

1. A treasure is our tongue that surges
   From deep shadows of the past,
   Chain of precious stones that scattered
   All over our ancient land.
   A burning flame is our tongue
   Amidst a people waking
   From a deathly sleep, no warning,
   Like the brave man of the stories.
   Our tongue is made of songs
   From our soul's deepest desires,
   Flash of lightning striking swiftly
   Through dark clouds and blue horizons.

2. Our tongue is the tongue of bread
   When the winds blow through the summer,
   Uttered by our forefathers who
   Blessed the country through their labour.
   Our tongue is the greenest leaf
   Of the everlasting forests,
   Gentle river Nistru's ripples
   Hiding starlight bright and shining.
   Utter no more bitter cries now
   That your language is too poor,
   And you will see with what abundance
   Flow the words of our precious country.

3. Our tongue is full of legends,
   Stories from the days of old.
   Reading one and then another
   Makes one shudder, tremble and moan.
   Our tongue is singled out
   To lift praises up to heaven,
   Uttering with constant fervour
   Truths that never cease to beckon.
   Our tongue is more than holy,
   Words of homilies of old
   Wept and sung perpetually
   In the homesteads of our folks.

4. Resurrect now this our language,
   Rusted through the years that have passed,
   Wipe off filth and mould that gathered
   When forgotten through our land.
   Gather now the sparkling stone,
   Catching bright light from the sun.
   You will see the endless flooding
   Of new words that overflow.
   A treasure will spring up swiftly
   From deep shadows of the past,
   Chain of precious stones that scattered
   All over our ancient land.

MONACO

Words by
THÉOPHILE BELLANDO de CASTRO (1820 - 1903)

Music by
CHARLES ALBRECHT (1817 - 1895)
Arr. by W. L. REED

1. Prin - ci - pau - té Mo - na - co ma pa - tri - e,

Performed for the first time in 1867. The music is based on a folk song used to Bellando's words as a marching song by the Guarde Nationale, in which Bellando served as a captain.

2. *Fiers Compagnons de la Garde Civique,*
   Respectons tous la voix du Commandant.
   Suivons toujours notre bannière antique.
   Le tambour bat, marchons tous en Avant,
   Le tambour bat, marchons tous en Avant.

3. *Oui, Monaco connut toujours des braves.*
   Nous sommes tous leurs dignes descendants.
   En aucun temps nous ne fûmes esclaves,
   Et loin de nous, régnèrent les tyrans,
   Et loin de nous, régnèrent les tyrans.

4. *Que le nom d'un Prince plein de clémence*
   Soit repété par mille et mille chants.
   Nous mourons tous pour sa propre défense,
   Mais après nous, combattront nos enfants,
   Mais après nous, combattront nos enfants.

Translation

1. Principality of Monaco, my country,
   Oh! how God is lavish with you.
   An ever-clear sky, ever-blossoming shores,
   Your Sovereign is better liked than a King,
   Your Sovereign is better liked than a King.

2. Proud Fellows of the Civic Guard,
   Let us all listen to the Commander's voice.
   Let us always follow our ancient flag.
   Drums are beating, let us all march forward,
   Drums are beating, let us all march forward.

3. Yes, Monaco always had brave men.
   We all are their worthy descendants.
   We never were slaves,
   And far from us ruled the tyrants,
   And far from us ruled the tyrants.

4. Let the name of a Prince full of clemency
   Be repeated in thousands and thousands of songs.
   We shall all die in his defence,
   But after us, our children will fight,
   But after us, our children will fight.

MONGOLIA

Words by
TSENDIIN DAMDINSUREN (1908 - 1986)

Music by
BILEGIIN DAMDINSUREN (1919 -1991)
and LUVSANJAMTS MURJORJ (1915 - 1996)

1. Dar khan ma nai khuvs galt u - l(a)s

Da - laar mongo-lyn a - riun go - lom - t(oo)

Dais - ny khold khe - zeech o - rokh-gui

The music was adopted in 1950, and the original words in 1961. New words were written in 1991.

Khair - t(ai) mon - gol or - noo man - duul - iaa._____

2. *Zorigt mongolyn zoltoi arduud*
   Zovlong tonilgozh zhargalyg edlev
   Zhargalyn tulkhuur khogzhliin tulguur
   Zhavkhlant manai oron mandtugai.

   CHORUS

Translation by D. Altangorel

1. Our sacred revolutionary country
   Is the ancestral hearth of all Mongols,
   No enemy will defeat us,
   And we will prosper for eternity.

   CHORUS
   Our country will strengthen relations
   With all righteous countries of the world.
   And let us develop our beloved Mongolia
   With all our will and might.

2. The glorious people of the brave Mongolia
   Have defeated all sufferings, and gained happiness,
   The key to delight, and the path to progress –
   Majestic Mongolia – our country, live forever!

   CHORUS

MOROCCO

Words by
ALI SQUALLI HOUSSAINI (*b.* 1932)

Music by
LÉO MORGAN (1919 - 1984)
Arr. by W. L. REED

The National Anthem of Morocco is also used in Western Sahara.

Mil'———— Kull Ja - na - aan   Thi - kr— Kull Li - san

Bil - ro - oh Bil - ja - sad Hab - ba Fa - ta - ak Lab - baa Ni - da - ak

Fi   Fam - mee Wa Fi Dam - mee Ha - waak Tha - r Noor Wa Naar——

Ikh - wa - tee Hay - yaa   Lil - a - la Saa - yee - a

Nush - hid Ad - dun - ya   An - na Hu - na— Nu - hay -

ya   Bi - sha' - aar   Al - lah   Al - Wa - tan   Al - Ma - lek.

Translation

Fountain of Freedom   Source of Light
    Where sovereignty and safety meet,
Safety and sovereignty   May you ever combine!
You have lived among nations   With title sublime,
Filling each heart,   Sung by each tongue,
Your champion has risen   And answered your call.
In my mouth   And in my blood
Your breezes have stirred   Both light and fire.
Up! my brethren,   Strive for the highest.
We call to the world   That we are here ready.
    We salute as our emblem
    God, Homeland and King.

MOZAMBIQUE

Words and music by
JUSTINO SIGAULANE CHEMANE (*b.* 1923)
Arr. by W. L. REED

1. Vi - va, vi - va a FRE - LI - MO, Gui - a do Po - vo Mo - çam - bi - ca - no! Po - vo he - ró - i - co qu' ar - ma em

Adopted in 1975, when the country became independent. A new National Anthem is expected.

nua e sem - pre ven - ce - rá._____

CHORUS

Vi - va Mo - çam - bi - que! Vi - va a Ban - dei - ra, sím-

bo - lo Na - cio - nal! Vi - va Mo - çam - bi - que! Que por

(rall. 2nd time)

ti o Po - vo lu - ta - rá._____ rá._____

2. *Unido ao mundo inteiro,*
   Lutando contra a burguesia,
   Nossa Pátria será túmulo
   Do capitalismo e exploração.
   O Povo Moçambicano
   D'operários e de camponeses,
   Engajado no trabalho
   A riqueza sempre brotará.

   CHORUS

Translation

1. Long live FRELIMO,
   Guide of the Mozambican people,
   Heroic people who, gun in hand,
       toppled colonialism.
   All the People united
   From the Rovuma to the Maputo,
   Struggle against imperialism
   And continue, and shall win.

   CHORUS
   Long live Mozambique!
   Long live our flag, symbol of the Nation!
   Long live Mozambique!
   For thee your People will fight.

2. United with the whole world,
   Struggling against the bourgeoisie,
   Our country will be the tomb
   Of capitalism and exploitation.
   The Mozambican People,
   Workers and peasants,
   Engaged in work
   Shall always produce wealth.

   CHORUS

MYANMAR

Words and music by
SAYA TIN (1914 - 1947)
Arr. by W. L. REED

This officially became the National Anthem in 1948.

* Bma (Burma - the former name of the country) is, pending official information to the contrary, retained in the original text and English translation.

Translation by T. M. Cartledge

We shall always love Burma, } (twice)
Land of our forefathers.
We fight and give our lives
For our union.
For her we responsibly shoulder the task,
Standing as one in duty to our precious land.

* The notes between asterisks may be sung an octave higher.
★ At the end of the National Anthem it is customary for the singers to give a slight bow.

NAMIBIA

Words and music by
AXALI DOESEB (*b.* 1954)
Arr. by W. L. REED

Na - mi - bi - a, land— of the brave, Free - dom's fight we have won. Glo - ry to their— bra - ve - ry, Whose blood wa - ters our free - dom. We— give our love and loy - al - ty

Adopted on 21 March, 1991, first anniversary of independence.

NAURU

Words written collectively

Music by
LAURENCE HENRY HICKS (*b.* 1912)
Arr. by W. L. REED

Nau - ru bwi - e - ma, nga - ben - a ma au - we. Ma de - da - ro bwe do - gum, mo o - ta - ta bet eg - om. A - tsin nga - go bwi -

Officially adopted in 1968, when the country obtained independence.

yin ou - ge, Nau - ru e - ko do - gin!

Translation

Nauru our homeland, the land we dearly love,
We all pray for you and we also praise your name.
Since long ago you have been the home of our great forefathers
And will be for generations yet to come.
We all join in together to honour your flag,
And we shall rejoice together and say;
Nauru for evermore!

NEPAL

Words by
CHAKRAPANI CHALISE (1884 - 1959)

Music by
BAKHATBIR BUDHAPIRTHI (1857 - 1920)

Shri mân gum - bhi - ra ne - pâ - li pra-chan-da pra-tâ-
pi bhu-pa-ti Shri pânch sar - kâr ma-hâ - râ -
jâ-dhi-râ-ja ko sa-dâ ra-hos un-na-ti Ra - khun chi râ-yu ee-sha-

Music adopted in 1899. Words adopted in 1924.

le pra - jâ phai - li - yos pu - kâ - raun ja - ya pre - ma - le Hâ -

mi ne - pâ - li bhâ - ee_____ sâ - râ - le.

rall.

Translation

May glory crown you, courageous Sovereign,
You, the gallant Nepalese,
Shri Pansh Maharajadhiraja, our glorious ruler,
May he live for many years to come
And may the number of his subjects increase.
Let every Nepalese sing this with joy.

NETHERLANDS

Words by
PHILIP VAN MARNIX OF ST. ALGEGONDE (1540 - 1598)

Composer unknown*
Arr. by M. J. BRISTOW

Broad

1. Wil - hel - mus van Nas - sou - we Ben ick van Duit - schen

bloet; Den Va - der - lant ghe - trou - we Blijf ick tot in den

doet. Een prin - ce van O - ran - jen Ben ick

Officially adopted on 10 May, 1932. There are fifteen verses in all. The National Anthem of the Netherlands is also used in Aruba and the Netherlands Antilles.
*Melody known from before 1572. Song appeared in Valerius *Nederlandtsche Gedenck - Clanck*, 1626.

2. *Mijn schilt ende betrouwen*
   Zijt ghy, O Godt, mijn Heer,
   Op U soo wil ick bouwen,
   Verlaet my nimmermeer;
   Dat ick doch vroom mag blijven
   U dienaer t'aller stond,
   Die tyranny verdrijven,
   Die my mijn hert doorwondt.

Translation by T. M. Cartledge

1. William of Nassau am I, of Germanic descent;
   True to the fatherland I remain until death.
   Prince of Orange am I, free and fearless.
   To the King of Spain I have always given honour.

2. You, my God and Lord, are my shield, on You I rely.
   On You I will build; never leave me,
   So that I may remain pious, Your servant at all moments,
   Dispelling the tyranny that wounds my heart.

NEW ZEALAND
God Defend New Zealand

English words by
THOMAS BRACKEN (1843 - 1898)
Maori words by
THOMAS HENRY SMITH (1824 - 1907)

Music by
JOHN JOSEPH WOODS (1849 - 1934)

Officially adopted in Centennial Year, 1940. This National Anthem and the National Anthem of the United Kingdom were given equal status in 1977, as New Zealand's National Anthems. The National Anthem of New Zealand is also used in Niue and Tokelau. The Cook Islands have their own National Anthem.

Make her prais - es heard a - far, God de - fend New Zea - land.
Ma - na - a - ki - ti - a mai A - o - te - a - ro - a.

13

2. Men of every creed and race
   Gather here before Thy face,
   Asking Thee to bless this place,
   God defend our free land.
   From dissension, envy, hate
   And corruption guard our State,
   Make our country good and great,
   God defend New Zealand.

3. Peace, not war, shall be our boast,
   But, should foes assail our coast,
   Make us then a mighty host,
   God defend our free land.
   Lord of battles, in Thy might,
   Put our enemies to flight,
   Let our cause be just and right,
   God defend New Zealand.

4. Let our love for Thee increase,
   May Thy blessings never cease,
   Give us plenty, give us peace,
   God defend our free land.
   From dishonour and from shame
   Guard our country's spotless name,
   Crown her with immortal fame,
   God defend New Zealand.

5. May our mountains ever be
   Freedom's ramparts on the sea,
   Make us faithful unto Thee,
   God defend our free land.
   Guide her in the nations' van,
   Preaching love and truth to man,
   Working out Thy glorious plan,
   God defend New Zealand.

2. *Ona mano tangata*
   Kiri whero, kiri ma,
   Iwi Maori Pakeha,
   Repeke katoa,
   Nei ka tono ko nga he
   Mau e whakaahu ke,
   Kia ora marire
   Aotearoa.

3. *Tona mana kia tu!*
   Tona kaha kia u;
   Tona rongo hei paku
   Ki te ao katoa,
   Aua rawa nga whawhai,
   Nga tutu a tata mai,
   Kia tupu nui ai
   Aotearoa.

4. *Waiho tona takiwa*
   Ko te ao marama;
   Kia whiti tona ra
   Taiawhio noa.
   Ko te hae me te ngangau
   Meinga kia kore kau;
   Waiho i te rongo mau
   Aotearoa.

5. *Tona pai toitu;*
   Tika rawa, pono pu;
   Tona noho, tana tu;
   Iwi no Ihoa.
   Kaua mona whakama;
   Kia hau te ingoa;
   Kia tu hei tauira;
   Aotearoa.

NICARAGUA

Words by
SALOMÓN IBARRA MAYORGA (1890 - 1985)

Music by
LUIS ABRAHAM DELGADILLO (1887 - 1961)

Sal-ve a ti Ni - ca - ra - gua en tu sue - lo, Ya no ru - ge la voz__ del cañ-ón Ni__ se ti - ñe con san - gre de her-

The words formerly sung were replaced by these words in 1939 by a government decree.

ma - nos Tu glo - rio - so pen - dón___ bi - co-

lor,___ Ni se ti - ñe con san - gre de her - ma-nos Tu glo-

rio - so pen - dón___ bi - co - lor. Bri - lle her-

mo - sa la paz___ en tu cie - lo, Na - da em-pa - ñe tu

glo - ria in - mor - tal Que el tra - ba - jo es tu dig - no lau -

rel Y— el ho - nor——— es tu en - se - ña tri - un - fal,———

— es tu en - se - ña tri - un - fal.

Translation by T. M. Cartledge

Hail to you, Nicaragua.
The cannon's voice no longer roars,
Nor does the blood of our brothers
Stain your glorious bicoloured flag. } (twice)
Peace shines in beauty in your skies,
Nothing dims your immortal glory,
For work is what earns your laurels
And honour is your triumphal ensign.

NIGER

Words by
MAURICE ALBERT THIRIET (1906 - 1969)

Music by
ROBERT JACQUET (1896 - 1976) and
NICOLAS ABEL FRANÇOIS FRIONNET (*b.* 1911)

1. Au - près du grand Ni - ger puis - sant   Qui rend la na - tu - re plus bel - le,

So - yons fiers et re - con - nais - sants   De no - tre li - ber - té nou - vel - le.

Niger became fully independent in 1960. Approved by the National Assembly in July, 1961.

E - vi - tons les vai - nes que - rel - les A - fin d'é - par - gner no - tre sang;

Et que les glo - rieux ac - cents De no - tre ra - ce sans tu - tel - le S'é-

lèvent dans un mê - me é - lan Jus - qu'à ce ciel é - blou - is - sant Où

veil - le son âme é - ter - nel - le Qui fe - ra le pa - ys plus grand.___ De -

bout Ni - ger: De - bout!_____ Sur le sol et sur l'on - de, Au

ryth - me des tam - tams, dans leur son gran - dis - sant, Res -

tons u - nis, tou - jours,____ et que cha - cun ré - pon - de A ce noble a - ve -

poco rall.

nir qui nous dit: "En____ a - vant."____

2. *Nous retrouvons dans nos enfants*
   Toutes les vertus des Ancêtres:
   Pour lutter dans tous les instants
   Elles sont notre raison d'être.
   Nous affrontons le fauve traître
   A peine armés le plus souvent,
   Voulant subsister dignement
   Sans detruire pour nous repaître.
   Dans la steppe où chacun ressent
   La soif, dans le Sahel brûlant,
   Marchons, sans défaillance, en maîtres
   Magnanimes et vigilants.

CHORUS

Translation by T. M. Cartledge

1. By the waters of the mighty Niger,
   Which adds to the beauty of nature,
   Let us be proud and grateful
   For our new-won liberty.
   Let us avoid vain quarrelling,
   So that our blood may be spared,
   And may the glorious voice
   Of our race, free from tutelage,
   Rise unitedly, surging as from one man,
   To the dazzling skies above,
   Where its eternal soul, watching over us,
   Brings greatness to the country.

   CHORUS
   Arise, Niger, arise! May our fruitful work
   Rejuvenate the heart of this old continent,
   And may this song resound around the world,
   Like the cry of a just and valiant people.
   Arise, Niger, arise! On land and river,
   To the rhythm of the swelling drum-beats' sound,
   May we ever be united and may each one of us
   Answer the call of this noble future that says to us, 'Forward!'

2. We find again in our children
   All the virtues of our ancestors.
   Such virtues are our inspiration
   For fighting at every moment.
   We confront ferocious and treacherous animals
   Often scarcely armed,
   Seeking to live in dignity,
   Not slaying with a lust to kill.
   In the steppe where all feel thirst,
   In the burning desert,
   Let us march tirelessly forward
   As magnanimous and vigilant masters.

   CHORUS

NIGERIA

Words written collectively

Music by
BENEDICT ELIDE ODIASE (*b.* 1934)
Arr. by W. L. REED

Adopted in 1978.

vain, To serve with heart and might One na - tion bound— in

free - dom,—— peace and u - ni - ty.

2. O God of creation,
Direct our noble cause;
Guide Thou our leaders right:
Help our Youth the truth to know,
In love and honesty to grow,
And living just and true,
Great lofty heights attain,
To build a nation where peace and justice reign.

NORWAY

Words by
BJØRNSTJERNE BJØRNSON (1832 - 1910)

Music by
RIKARD NORDRAAK (1842 - 1866)

Ja, vi el - sker det - te lan - det Som det sti - ger frem,

Fu - ret, vær - bitt o - ver van - net Med de tu - sen hjem.

El - sker, el - sker det og ten - ker På vår far og mor Og den

The words were first published in 1859 and the music probably composed in 1863 or 1864. First performed on 17 May, 1864 to celebrate the 50th anniversary of the Norwegian Constitution. There are eight verses.

saga-natt som sen - ker Drøm - me på vår jord, Og den

saga-natt som sen - ker, Sen - ker drøm - me på vår jord!

2. Norske mann i hus og hytte,
   Takk din store Gud!
   Landet ville han beskytte,
   Skjønt det mørkt så ut.
   Alt, hva fedrene har kjempet,
   Mødrene har grett,
   Har den Herre stille lempet,
   Så vi vant vår rett,
   Har den Herre stille lempet,
   Så vi vant, vi vant vår rett.

3. Ja, vi elsker dette landet,
   Som det stiger frem,
   Furet, værbitt over vannet,
   Med de tusen hjem!
   Og som fedres kamp har hevet
   Det av nød til seir,
   Også vi, når det blir krevet,
   For dets fred slår leir,
   Også vi, nar det blir krevet,
   For dets fred, dets fred slår leir!

Translation by Hilde Midttømme and T. M. Cartledge

1. Yes, we love this country
   Which rises up,
   Rugged and weathered, above the sea,
   With its thousands of homes.
   Love it, love it and think
   About our mothers and fathers
   And the saga of past ages
   That sends dreams to our earth,
   And the saga of past ages
   That sends dreams, sends dreams to our earth.

2. Norsemen, in house and cabin,
   Thank your great God!
   It was His will to protect the country
   Although things looked dark.
   While fathers fought
   And mothers cried,
   Our Lord quietly opened the way
   So that we won our right.
   Our Lord quietly opened the way
   So that we won, we won our right.

3. Yes, we love this country
   Which rises up,
   Rugged and weathered, above the sea,
   With its thousands of homes.
   And as our fathers' struggle has raised it
   From distress to victory,
   We also, when called upon,
   Will strike a blow for its peace.
   We also, when called upon,
   Will strike a blow for its peace, its peace.

OMAN

Author unknown

Composer unknown
Arr. by RODNEY BASHFORD
and W. L. REED

Ya Rab-ba-na Eh-fid La-na Ja-la-lat Al Sul-tan Wa-a-sha-bi Fee Al'w-tan Bi al-

Muscat and Oman became Oman in 1970. The National Anthem has been in use since 1972.

fiya   Min   K'ram   Al   A   -   ra   -   bi.   Ab-   shi-   ry   Qa-   boos   Ja-   a   Fal   -   tu-

ba   -   ra   -   khu   'I   Sa   -   ma.   Waa   -   si   -   dy   Wal   -   to   -   q'hi   Bil   -   duo-   aa,

Translation

O Lord, protect for us our Majesty the Sultan
And the people in our land,
With honour and peace.

May he live long, strong and supported,
Glorified be his leadership.   } (twice)
For him we shall lay down our lives.

O Oman, since the time of the Prophet
We are a dedicated people amongst the noblest Arabs.
Be happy! Qaboos has come
With the blessings of Heaven.

Be cheerful and commend him to the protection of your prayers.

PAKISTAN

Words by
ABU-AL-ASAR HAFEEZ JULLANDHURI (1900 - 1982)

Music by
AHMED GHULAMALI CHAGLA (1902 - 1953)
Arr. by BRYSON GERRARD

Music officially accepted, December 1953. Words officially accepted, August 1954.

zam   qu - wa-te   a-khu - wa-te   a - wam

Qaum, mulk, Sul - ta-nat   Pain - da ta bin-da bad   shad, bad___ man ze-le mu-

rad.   3. Par - cham - e   si - ta - ra - o   hi - lal

Rah - ba-re   tar-ra - qi-o   ka mal   Tar-ju - ma-ne   ma - zi - sha - ne

hal ja - ne is - taq - bal Say - yai, khu - dae zul ja - lal.

Translation

1. Blessed be the sacred land,
   Happy be the bounteous realm,
   Symbol of high resolve,
   Land of Pakistan.
   Blessed be thou citadel of faith.

2. The Order of this Sacred Land
   Is the might of the brotherhood of the people.
   May the nation, the country, and the State
   Shine in glory everlasting.
   Blessed be the goal of our ambition.

3. This flag of the Crescent and the Star
   Leads the way to progress and perfection,
   Interpreter of our past,glory of our present,
   Inspiration of our future,
   Symbol of Almighty's protection.

415

PALAU

Words by
Several authors

Music by
YMESEI O. EZEKIEL (1926 - 1984)
Arr. by W. L. REED

1. Be - lau lo - ba kli - siich er a kelu - lul,

El di - mia ngar - ngii ra re - chuo - del - mei

Meng —— me - ngel uoluu er a chi - mol be - luu,

Officially adopted on 25 December, 1980.

416

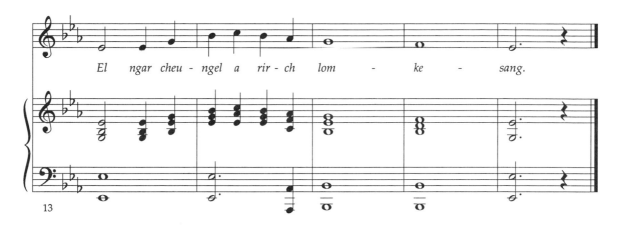

El ngar cheu - ngel a rir - ch lom - ke - sang.

2. Bo dole ketek a kerruul er a belluad,
   Iolab a blakelreng ma duchelreng.
   Belau a chotil a klengar er kid,
   Mebo dorurtabedul msa klisichel.

3. Bod kai ue reked chim lokiu a reng,
   E dongedmokel radimla koted.
   Lomcheliu a rengedel ma klebkellel,
   Iokiu a budch ma beltikelreng.

4. Dios mo mek ngel tengat ra Be lumam,
   El dimla dikesam ra rechuodelmei.
   Beskemam a klisicham ma llemeltam,
   Iorrurt a klungiolam elmo ch'rechar.

Translation

1. Palau is coming forth with strength and power,
   By her old ways abides still every hour.
   One country, safe, secure, one government
   Under the glowing, floating soft light stands.

2. Let's build our economy's protecting fence
   With courage, faithfulness and diligence.
   Our life is anchored in Palau our land.
   We with our might through life and death defend.

3. In spirit let's join hands, united, one;
   Care for our homeland, from forefathers on.
   Look after its concord, its glory keep.
   Through peace and love and heart's devotion deep.

4. God bless our country, our Island Home always.
   Our sweet inheritance from ancient days.
   Give us the strength and power and all the right
   To govern well to all eternity.

PANAMA

Words by
JERÓNIMO DE LA OSSA (1847 - 1907)

Music by
SANTOS JORGE (1870 - 1941)
Arr. by MARTIN SHAW

Used for the first time on 4 November, 1903, when the people carried the flag of the new Republic through the streets of the capital. It was officially adopted in 1925.

dien - tes ful - go - res de glo - ria Se ilu -

mi - na la nue - va Na - ción, Con ar - dien - tes ful - go - res de

FINE

glo - ria Se ilu - mi - na la nue - va Na - ción.

FINE

Meno mosso
p dolce

p dolce e legato

1. Es pre - ci - so cu - brir con un ve - lo Del pa -

sa - do el Cal - va - rio y la Cruz,_____ Y que a-dor - ne el a-zul de tu

ciel - o, De con - cor - dia la es - plén - di - da luz. El pro-

gre - so a - ca - ri - cia tus la - res Al com - pás de su - bli - me can-

ción; Ves ru - gir a tus pies am - bos ma - res, Que dan

rum - bo a tu no - ble mi - sión.

D. 𝄋 al Fine

2. *En tu suelo cubierto de flores,*
   A los besos del tibio terral,
   Terminaron guerreros fragores,
   Sólo reina el amor fraternal.
   Adelante la pica y la pala,
   Al trabajo sin más dilación:
   Y seremos así prez y gala
   De este mundo feraz de Colón.

   CHORUS

Translation by T. M. Cartledge

CHORUS
We finally attained victory
In the happy field of union.
With glowing splendour,
The new nation is illumined.   } (twice)

1. It is necessary to veil with a curtain
   The Calvary and Cross of the past,
   And for you to adorn the azure of your skies
   With the splendid light of concord.
   Progress fondly touches your homes,
   In time with the music of a sublime song.
   You see, roaring at your feet, two oceans
   Which give direction to your noble mission.

   CHORUS

2. On your flower-covered soil,
   Kissed by the warm breeze,
   Warlike clamour has ended
   And only brotherly love reigns.
   Ahead, with spade and stone-mason's hammer!
   To work, without more delay!
   In this way we shall be the honour and glory
   Of this fertile land of Columbus.

   CHORUS

PAPUA NEW GUINEA

Words and music by
THOMAS SHACKLADY (*b.* 1917)
Arr. by W. L. REED

1. O a - rise all you sons of this land, Let us

sing of our joy to be free, Prais - ing God and re - joic - ing to

be Pa - pu - a New Gui - nea. Shout our name from the moun - tains to

Adopted in 1975, when the country became independent.

seas. Pa - pu - a New Gui - nea; Let us

raise our voi-ces and pro-claim Pa - pu - a——— New Gui - nea.

rall.

2. Now give thanks to the good Lord above
   For His kindness, His wisdom and love
   For this land of our fathers so free,
   Papua New Guinea.

   CHORUS
   Shout again for the whole world to hear
   Papua New Guinea;
   We're independent and we're free,
   Papua New Guinea.

PARAGUAY

Words by
FRANCISCO ESTEBAN
  ACUÑA DE FIGUEROA (1791 - 1862) *

Music by
FRANCISCO JOSÉ DEBALI (1791 - 1859)†
or FRANCÉS DUPUY (1813 - 1861)
or LOUIS CAVEDAGNI (*d.* 1916)#
Transcribed by
REMBERTO GIMÉNEZ

Adopted in 1846. This present arrangement was declared the official version in May 1934. There are seven verses.
* Francisco Esteban Acuña de Figueroa also wrote the words of the National Anthem of Uruguay.
†Francisco José Debali also composed the music of the National Anthem of Uruguay.
Date of birth unknown.

brí - o nos dió___ li - ber - tad;_____ Ni o - pre -

so - res, ni sier - vos, a - lien - tan, Don - de

re - i - nan u - nión, e i - gual - dad._____ Ni o - pre -

so - res, ni sier - vos, a - lien - tan, Don - de

429

Translation by T. M. Cartledge

VERSE

For three centuries a reign oppressed
The unhappy peoples of America,
But one day, their anger aroused, they said:
"An end to this!" and broke the reign.
Our forefathers, fighting magnificently,
Displayed their martial glory,
And when the august diadem was shattered,
They raised the triumphal cap of liberty. } (twice)

CHORUS

Paraguayans, Republic or death!
It was our strength that gave us our final liberty.
Neither tyrants nor slaves can continue,
Where unity and equality reign, } (twice)
Where unity and equality reign.

PERU

Words by
JOSÉ DE LA TORRE UGARTE (1786 - 1831)

Music by
JOSÉ BERNARDO ALZEDO (1788 - 1878)
Arr. by HENRY COLEMAN

Words and music chosen as result of a competition promoted by General San Martín in 1821. They were declared official on 12 February, 1913. There are six verses.

grado ¡Li-ber-tad! en sus cos-tas— se o-yó, La in-do-

35

cresc.
len-cia de es-cla-vo sa-cu — de, La hu-mi-lla-da, la hu-mi-

38

cresc.
lla-da, la hu-mi-lla-da cer-viz le-van-tó,— La hu-mi-

41

p   rall. molto   cresc.   a tempo
                                              D. % al Fine
lla-da cer-viz— le-van-tó, cer-viz— le-van-tó.— So-mos

44

Translation

CHORUS
We are free; let us always be so,
And let the sun rather deny its light
Than that we should fail the solemn vow
Which our country raised to God.

VERSE
For a long time the Peruvian, oppressed,
Dragged the ominous chain;
Condemned to cruel serfdom,
For a long time he moaned in silence.
But as soon as the sacred cry of
Freedom! was heard on his coasts,
He shook off the indolence of the slave,
He raised his humiliated head.

CHORUS

THE PHILIPPINES

Words (Tagalog version) by
FELIPE PADILLA DE LEON (1912 - 1992)

Music by
JULIAN FELIPE (1861 - 1944)

First performed in conjunction with the reading of the Act of Proclamation of Independence, 12 June, 1898. The music was composed in 1898, and the original Spanish words were written in 1899 by José Palma (1876 - 1903). Tagolog version officially adopted in 1935. Spanish ceased to be an official language in 1973.

Sa man - lu - lu - pig Di ka pa - si - si - il.

3. Sa da - gat at bun - dok, Sa si - moy, at sa la - ngit mong bug -

haw, May di - lag ang tu - la, At a - wit sa pag -

la - yang mi - na - ma - hal. 4. Ang kis - lap ng wa - ta wat

mo'y Ta - gum - pay na nag - ni - ning - ning, Ang bi - tu -

in at a - raw niya, Kai - lan pa ma'y di mag - di - di -

lim. 5. Lu - pa ng a - raw ng lu - wal -

ha - tit pag - sin - ta, Bu - hay ay la - ngit sa pi - ling

mo. A - ming li ga - ya na pag ma'y

mang — a - a - pi Ang ma - ma - tay nang

da hil sa iyo.

D.C. al Fine

Original words written in Spanish

1. *Tierra adorada,*
   Hija del sol de Oriente,
   Su fuego ardiente
   En ti latiendo está.

2. *Tierra de amores,*
   Del heróismo cuna,
   Los invasores
   No te hollarán jamás.

3. *En tu azul cielo, en tus auras,*
   En tus montes y en tu mar
   Esplende y late el poema
   De tu amada libertad.

4. *Tu pabellón que en las lides*
   La victoria iluminó,
   No verá nunca apagados
   Sus estrellas ni su sol.

5. *Tierra de dichas, de sol y amores,*
   En tu regazo dulce es vivir;
   Es una gloria para tus hijos,
   Cuando te ofenden, por ti morir.

   Repeat verses 1 & 2.

Translation by T. M. Cartledge from the Spanish

1. Beloved land,
   Daughter of the eastern sun,
   Your heart is beating
   With ardent fire.

2. Land of love,
   Cradle of heroism,
   Invaders shall never
   Trample on you.

3. In your blue sky and gentle breezes,
   In your mountains and sea,
   The epic of your beloved freedom
   Shines and throbs.

4. Your banner, which has illuminated
   Victory in battle,
   Will never see its stars
   Or its sun blotted out.

5. Land of good fortune, sun and love,
   It is sweet to live in your embrace;
   It is a glory for your sons
   To die for you when you are wronged.

   Repeat verses 1 & 2.

440

POLAND

Words by
JÓZEF WYBICKI (1747 - 1822)

Music by
MICHAL KLEOFAS OGIŃSKI (1765 - 1833)
This is not certain
Arr. by W. L. REED

This song, first sung in 1795, was a favourite with the Polish Legions in the Napoleonic wars. In 1927 it was authorised as its National Anthem by the new Polish republican government. The melody resembles that of the National Anthem of Yugoslavia (Serbia and Montenegro)

Za two-im prze - wo - dem złac-zym się z na - ro - dem.

2. *Przejdziem Wisłę, przejdziem Wartę,*
   Będziem Polakami,
   Dat nam przykład Bonaparte
   Jak zwyciężać mamy.

   CHORUS

3. *Jak Czarniecki do Poznania*
   Po szwedzkim zaborze,
   Dla ojczyzny ratowania
   Wrócim się przez morze.

   CHORUS

Translation by Jerzy Żebrowski

1. Poland has not yet succumbed.
   As long as we remain,
   What the foe by force has seized,
   Sword in hand we'll gain.

   CHORUS
   March! March, Dąbrowski!
   March from Italy to Poland!
   Under your command
   We shall reach our land.

2. Cross the Vistula and Warta
   And Poles we shall be;
   We've been shown by Bonaparte
   Ways to victory.

   CHORUS

3. As Czarniecki Poznań town regains,
   Fighting with the Swede,
   To free our fatherland from chains,
   We shall return by sea.

   CHORUS

PORTUGAL

Words by
HENRIQUE LOPES DE MENDONÇA (1856 - 1931)

Music by
ALFREDO KEIL (1850 - 1907)
Arr. by W. L. REED

First played in January, 1890. Approved as the National Anthem in 1910. The National Anthem of Portugal is also used in Macao.

ar - mas! Às ar - mas! Pe-la Pá - tria lu-

tar!＿＿＿＿ Con-tra_os ca - nhões mar - char, Mar - char!＿＿＿

2. Desfralda a invicta bandeira
   À luz viva do teu céu!
   Brade à Europa à terra inteira:
   Portugal não pereceu!
   Beija o solo teu jucundo
   O Oceano a rugir d'amor;
   E o teu braço vencedor
   Deu novos mundos ao mundo!

   CHORUS

3. Saudai o sol que desponta
   Sobre um ridente porvir;
   Seja o eco de uma afronta
   O sinal do ressurgir.
   Ráios dessa aurora forte
   São como beijos de mãe
   Que nos guardam, nos sustêm
   Contra as injúrias da sorte.

   CHORUS

Translation

1. Heroes of the sea, noble race,
   Valiant and immortal nation,
   Now is the hour to raise up on high once more
   Portugal's splendour.
   From out of the mists of memory,
   Oh Homeland, we hear the voices
   Of your great forefathers
   That shall lead you on to victory!

   CHORUS
   To arms, to arms
   On land and sea!
   To arms, to arms
   To fight for our Homeland!
   To march against the enemy guns!

2. Unfurl the unconquerable flag
   In the bright light of your sky!
   Cry out to all Europe and the whole world
   That Portugal has not perished.
   Your happy land is kissed
   By the Ocean that murmurs with love.
   And your conquering arm
   Has given new worlds to the world!

   CHORUS

3. Salute the Sun that rises
   On a smiling future:
   Let the echo of an insult be
   The signal for our revival.
   The rays of that powerful dawn
   Are like a mother's kisses
   That protect us and support us
   Against the insults of fate.

   CHORUS

QATAR

No words

Composer unknown *

Officially adopted in 1954.
* Music possibly of Indian origin.

ROMANIA

Words by
ANDREI MUREŞANU (1816 - 1863)

Music by
ANTON PANN (1796 - 1854)
Arr. by W. L. REED

1. Deş - teap - tă - te, ro - mâ - ne, din som - nul cel de moar - te În ca - re te-a - dîn - ci - ră bar - ba - rii de ti - runi,_____ bar - ba - rii___ de ti - rani! A - cum ori nici - o -

Adopted in April, 1990.

mani,_____ şi cru - zii__ tăi duş - mani! (Verses 2.3.4) mînt!

2. *Acum ori niciodată să dăm dovezi la lume*
   Că-n aste mîini mai curge un sînge de roman
   Şi că-n a noastre piepturi păstrăm cu fală-un nume
   Triumfător în lupte, un nume de Traian!

3. *Priviţi măreţe umbre, Mihai, Ştefan, Corvine,*
   Româna naţiune, ai voştri strănepoţi,
   Cu braţele armate, cu focul vostru-n vine,
   ,,Viaţă-n libertate ori moarte !" strigăm toţi.

4. *Preoţi cu crucea-n frunte! Căci oastea e creştină,*
   Deviza-i libertate şi scopul ei prea sfînt,
   Murim mai bine-n luptă, cu glorie deplină,
   Decît să fim sclavi iarăşi în vechiul nost pămînt!

Translation by Gabriel Gafita

1. Wake up, Romanian, from your deadly slumber,
   In which barbaric tyrants kept you so long by force!
   Now or never is the time for you to have a new fate,
   Which should command respect of even your cruel enemies.

2. Now or never is the time for us to prove to the entire world
   That in these arms a Roman blood still flows,
   And that in our hearts we proudly keep a name
   Triumphant in all battles, the name of Trajan.*

3. Behold, glorious shadows, Mihai, Stephen, Corvin,**
   That is the Romanian nation, your own great-grandsons,
   With weapons in their hands, your fire in their veins,
   All shouting, "We want to live in freedom, or else better die!"

4. Priests carry the cross ahead! The army is all Christian,
   Its banner is called freedom and its ideal is sacred,
   We'd rather die in battle, and do it in full glory,
   Than live again like slaves in our dear old land.

* Roman emperor who conquered Dacia in 106 A.D.
** Romanian princes of the three Romanian principalities, Walachia, Moldavia and Transylvania, in the 15th and 16th centuries.

RUSSIAN FEDERATION

No words

Music by
MIKHAIL IVANOVICH GLINKA (1804 - 1857)
Arr. by A. PETROV and W. L. REED

Russia became an independent state on 26 December, 1991, the date of the dissolution of the U.S.S.R. The melody is the 'Patriotic Song', composed by Glinka, presumably in 1833. He never returned to this work, hence its absence from his list of compositions.

RWANDA

Based on an old Rwandan Folk tune by a
group of Rwandans (Abanyuramatwi)*
Arr by W. L. REED

1. Rwa - nda rwa-cu, Rwa - nda gi-hu - gu cya-mbya - ye,

Nda - ku - ra - ta - n'i - shya - ka n'u - bu - twa - li.

I - yo ni - bu - ts'i - bi gwi wa - gi - ze ku - ge - z'u - bu,

Adopted by the National Assembly and sanctioned by the President of the Republic on 11 December, 1962, the year
when the country became independent.
* This was the name of a Choral Society, in Gitrama.

ho - ro, mu ku - li,   mu   bwi-ge-nge no mu bwu - mvi - ka-ne.

2. Impundu ni zivuge mu Rwandahose:
   Republika yaku y'ubuhake,
   Ubukolonize bwagiye nk'ifun'iheze.
   Shing'umuzi Demokarasi
   Waduhaye kwitorera abategetsi.
   Banyarwanda: abakuru
   Namw'abato mwizihiy'u Rwanda:
       Turubumbatire mu mahoro, mu kuli,
       Mu bwigenge no mu bwumvikane.

3. Bavuka Rwandamwese muvuz'impundu,
   Demokarasi yarwo iraganje.
   Twayiharaniye rwose twes'uko tungana.
   Gatutsi, Gatwa na gahutu
   Namwe banyarwanda bandi mwabyiyemeje,
   Independansi twatsindiye
   Twese hamwe tuyishyikire:
       Turubumbatire mu mahoro, mu kuli,
       Mu bwigenge no mu bwumvikane.

4. Nimucyo dusingiz'Ibendera ryacu.
   Arakabaho na Prezida wacu.
   Barakabahw'abaturage b'iki Gihugu.
   Intego yacu Banyarwanda
   Twishyire kandi twizane mu Rwanda rwacu.
   Twese hamwe, twung'ubumwe
   Nta mususu duter'imbere ko:
       Turubumbatire mu mahoro, mu kuli,
       Mu bwigenge no mu bwumvikane.

Translation

1. My Rwanda, land that gave me birth,
   Fearlessly, tirelessly, I boast of you!
   When I recall your achievements to this very day,
   I praise the pioneers who have brought in our unshakeable Republic.
   Brothers all, sons of this Rwanda of ours,
   Come, rise up all of you,
       Let us cherish her in peace and in truth,
       In freedom and in harmony!

2. Let the victory drums beat throughout all Rwanda!
   The Republic has swept away feudal bondage.
   Colonialism has faded away like a worn-out shoe.
   Democracy, take root!
   Through you we have chosen our own rulers.
   People of Rwanda, old and young, citizens all,
       Let us cherish her in peace and in truth,
       In freedom and in harmony!

3. Home-born Rwandans all, beat the victory drums!
   Democracy has triumphed in our land.
   All of us together we have striven for it arduously.
   Together we have decreed it- Tutsi, Twa, Hutu, with other racial elements,
   This hard-won Independence of ours,
   Let us all join to build it up!
       Let us cherish it in peace and in truth,
       In freedom and in harmony!

4. Come let us extol our Flag!
   Long live our President, long live the citizens of our land!
   Let this be our aim, people of Rwanda:
   To stand on our own feet, in our own right, by our own means.
   Let us promote unity and banish fear.
   Let us go forward together in Rwanda.
       Let us cherish her in peace and in truth,
       In freedom and in harmony!

SAINT KITTS AND NEVIS

Words and music by
KENRICK ANDERSON GEORGES (*b*. 1955)
Arr. by W. L. REED

Adopted in 1983.

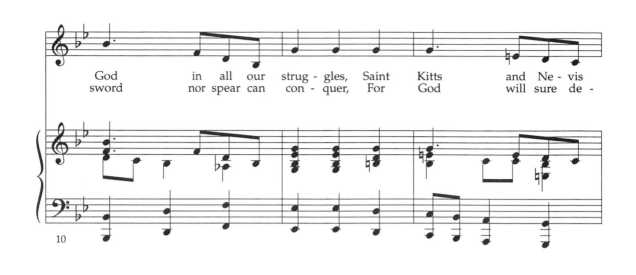

God   in all our strug - gles, Saint   Kitts   and Ne - vis
sword   nor spear can con - quer, For   God   will sure de -

be   A   Na - tion bound to - ge - ther With a
fend.   His   bless - ings shall for e - ver To pos -

com - mon des - ti - ny.   2. As stal - warts we stand, For
ter - i - ty   ex - tend.

FINE

D. % al Fine

SAINT LUCIA

Words by
CHARLES JESSE (1897 - 1985)

Music by
LETON FELIX THOMAS (*b.* 1926)
Arr. by W. L. REED

1. Sons and daugh-ters of Saint Lu - cia, Love the land that gave us birth, Land of bea - ches, hills and val - leys, Fair - est isle of— all the earth. Where - so - ev - er

Originally adopted in 1967 on achieving Statehood, and again in 1979 when becoming independent.

you may roam,—— Love, oh—— love your is - land home!

2. Gone the times when nations battled
   For this 'Helen of the West',
   Gone the days when strife and discord
   Dimmed her children's toil and rest.
   Dawns at last a brighter day,
   Stretches out a glad new way.

3. May the good Lord bless our island,
   Guard her sons from woe and harm!
   May our people live united,
   Strong in soul and strong in arm!
   Justice, Truth and Charity,
   Our ideal for ever be!

SAINT VINCENT AND THE GRENADINES

Words by
PHYLLIS JOYCE McCLEAN PUNNETT (*b.* 1917)

Music by
JOEL BERTRAM MIGUEL (*b.* 1938)
Arr. by W. L. REED

1. Saint Vin - cent! Land so beau - ti - ful, With joy - ful hearts we pledge to thee Our loy - al - ty and love, and vow To keep you e - ver free.

CHORUS

What - e'er the fu - ture brings, Our

Originally adopted in 1969 on achieving Statehood, and again in 1979 when becoming independent.

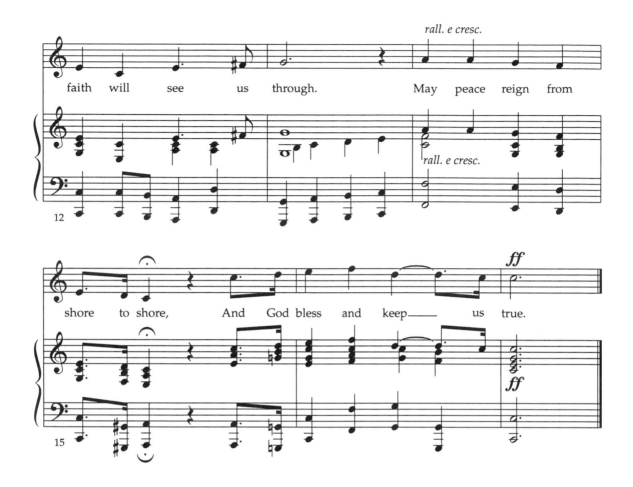

2. Hairoun! Our fair and blessed Isle,
   Your mountains high, so clear and green,
   Are home to me, though I may stray,
   A haven, calm, serene.

   CHORUS

3. Our little sister islands are
   Those gems, the lovely Grenadines,
   Upon their seas and golden sands
   The sunshine ever beams.

   CHORUS

SAN MARINO

No words *

Music by
FEDERICO CONSOLO (1841 - 1906)

Adopted in 1894. The music is based on a tenth century chorale from a breviary in the *Biblioteca Laurenziana*.
* There are no official words, though the Italian poet Giosué Carducci (1835 - 1907) has written a verse.

SÃO TOMÉ AND PRÍNCIPE

Words by
ALDA NEVES DA GRAÇA
DO ESPIRITO SANTO (*b.* 1926)

Music by
MANUEL DOS SANTOS BARRETO
DE SOUSA E ALMEIDA (*b.* 1933)
Arr. by W. L. REED

Translation by T. M. Cartledge

CHORUS
Independência total,
Glorioso canto do povo,
Independência total,
Hino sagrado de combate.
Dinamismo
Na luta nacional,
Juramento eterno
No país soberano de São Tomé e Príncipe.

1. *Guerrilheiro da guerra sem armas na mão,*
   Chama viva na alma do povo,
   Congregando os filhos das ilhas
   Em redor da Pátria Imortal.

2. *Independência total, total e completa,*
   Construindo, no progresso e na paz,
   A nação mais ditosa da Terra,
   Com os braços heróicos do povo.

   CHORUS
   Independência total,
   Glorioso canto do povo.
   Independência total,
   Hino sagrado de combate.

3. *Trabalhando, lutando, lutando e vencendo,*
   Caminhamos a passos gigantes
   Na cruzada dos povos africanos,
   Hasteando a bandeira nacional.

4. *Voz do povo, presente, presente em conjunto,*
   Vibra rijo no coro da esperança
   Ser herói no hora do perigo,
   Ser herói no ressurgir do País.

   CHORUS
   Independência total,
   Glorioso canto do povo,
   Independência total,
   Hino sagrado de combate.
   Dinamismo
   Na luta nacional,
   Juramento eterno
   No pais soberano de São Tomé e Príncipe.

CHORUS
Total independence,
Glorious song of the people,
Total independence,
Sacred hymn of combat.
Dynamism
In the national struggle,
Eternal oath
To the sovereign country of São Tomé and Príncipe.

1. Warriors in the war without weapons,
   Live flame in the soul of the people,
   Congregating the sons of the islands
   Around the Immortal Fatherland.

2. Total independence, total and complete,
   Building, in progress and peace,
   With the heroic hands of the people,
   The happiest nation on earth.

   CHORUS (first 4 lines only)

3. Working, struggling, struggling and conquering,
   We go ahead with giant steps
   In the crusade of the African peoples,
   Raising the national flag.

4. Voice of the people, present, present and united,
   Strong beat in the heart of hope
   To be a hero in the hour of peril,
   A hero of the Nation's resurgence.

   CHORUS (as at beginning)

467

SAUDI ARABIA

Words by
IBRAHIM KHAFAJI (*b.* 1935)

Music by
ABDUL RAHMAN AL-KHATEEB (*b.* 1923)
Arr. by W. L. REED

First performed in 1947, adopted in 1950.

Translation by M. A. S. Abdul Haleem

Hasten to glory and supremacy!
Glorify the Creator of the heavens
And raise the green, fluttering flag,
Carrying the emblem of Light!
Repeat - God is greatest!
O my country,
My country, may you always live,
The glory of all Muslims!
Long live the King,
For the flag and the country!

469

SÉNÉGAL

Words by
LÉOPOLD SÉDAR SENGHOR (b. 1906)*

Music by
HERBERT PEPPER (b. 1912)†

1. Pin - cez tous vos Ko - ras,# Frap - pez les ba - la - fons, Le

Lion rouge a ru - gi Le Domp - teur de la brousse d'un

Adopted in 1960, when the country became independent.
* The words are by the President, Léopold Sédar Senghor.
† Herbert Pepper also wrote the music for the National Anthem of the Central African Republic.
# The Kora is the harp-lute of the Sénégalese Griots.

bond s'est é - lan - cé Dis - si - pant les tén - è - bres. So -

leil sur nos ter - reurs, So - leil sur nos es - poirs.

De - bout frè - res, voi - ci l'A - fri - que ras - sem - blé - e.

CHORUS

Fi - bres de mon cœur vert, E - pau - le contre é - pau - le,

Mes plus que frères O Sé - né - ga - lais, de - bout!____

U - nis-sons la mer et les sour - ces, U - nis-sons la steppe et la fo - rêt. Sa -

1. lut Af - ri - que mè - re.

2. lut A - fri - que mère.

2. *Sénégal, toi le fils de l'écume du Lion,*
   Toi surgi de la nuit au galop des chevaux,
   Rends-nous, oh! rends-nous l'honneur de nos Ancêtres,
   Splendides comme ébène et forts comme le muscle
   Nous disons droits- l'épée n'a pas une bavure.

   CHORUS

3. *Sénégal, nous faisons nôtre ton grand dessein:*
   Rassembler les poussins à l'abri des milans
   Pour en faire, de l'Est à l'Ouest, du Nord au Sud,
   Dressé, un même peuple, un peuple sans couture
   Mais un peuple tourné vers tous les vents du monde.

   CHORUS

4. *Sénégal, comme toi, comme tous nos héros,*
   Nous serons durs sans haine et des deux bras ouverts.
   L'épée, nous la mettrons dans la paix du fourreau,
   Car le travail sera notre arme et la parole.
   Le Bantou est un frère, et l'Arabe et le Blanc.

   CHORUS

5. *Mais que si l'ennemi incendie nos frontières*
   Nous serons tous dressés et les armes au poing:
   Un Peuple dans sa foi défiant tous les malheurs,
   Les jeunes et les vieux, les hommes et les femmes.
   La Mort, oui! Nous disons la Mort, mais pas la honte.

   CHORUS

473

Translation by Elizabeth P. Coleman

1. Sound, all of you, your Koras,
   Beat the drums,
   The red Lion has roared,
   The Tamer of the bush with one leap has rushed forward
   Scattering the gloom.
   Light on our terrors,
   Light on our hopes.
   Arise, brothers, Africa behold united!

   CHORUS
   Shoulder to shoulder,
   O people of Sénégal, more than brothers to me, arise!
   Unite the sea and the springs,
   Unite the steppe and the forest!
   Hail, mother Africa,
   Hail, mother Africa!

2. Sénégal, thou son of the Lion
   Arise in the night with great speed,
   Restore, oh, restore to us the honour of our ancestors,
   Magnificent as ebony and strong as muscles!
   We are a straight people-the sword has no fault.

   CHORUS

3. Sénégal, we make your great design our own:
   To gather the chicks, sheltering them from kites,
   To make from them, from East to West, from North to South,
   A people rising as one, in seamless unity,
   Yet a people facing all the winds of the earth.

   CHORUS

4. Sénégal, like thee, like all our heroes,
   We will be stern without hatred, and with open arms.
   The sword we will put peacefully in its sheath,
   For work and words will be our weapon.
   The Bantu is our brother, the Arab, and the White man too.

   CHORUS

5. But if the enemy violates our frontiers,
   We will all be ready, weapons in our hands;
   A people in its faith defying all evil;
   Young and old, men and women,
   Death, yes! but not dishonour.

   CHORUS

SEYCHELLES

Koste Seselwa
(Seychellois, Unite!)

Words and music by
DAVID FRANÇOIS MARC ANDRÉ (*b.* 1958)
and GEORGE CHARLES ROBERT PAYET (*b.* 1959)
Arr. by W. L. REED

Officially adopted on 18 June, 1996, replacing the former National Anthem.

An - sanm pour tou le-ter-ni-té, Kos - te Se - sel - wa.

Translation

Seychelles, our homeland.
Where we live in harmony.
Joy, love and peace,
We thank God.
Let us preserve the beauty of our country
And the wealth of our oceans,
Which are both precious heritages
For the future of our children.
Let us stay in unity always
Under the colours of our new flag,
And together for eternity,
Seychellois, Unite!

SIERRA LEONE

Words by
CLIFFORD NELSON FYLE (*b.* 1933)

Music by
JOHN JOSEPH AKAR (1927 - 1975)
Arr. by HENRY COLEMAN

1. High we ex-alt— thee, realm of the free; Great is the love— we
have for— thee; Firm-ly u-nit-ed e-ver we stand,
Sing-ing thy praise,— O— nat-ive— land. We raise up our hearts and our

Written and composed in 1961 and adopted when the country achieved independence on 27 April, 1961.

2. One with a faith that wisdom inspires,
   One with a zeal that never tires;
   Ever we seek to honour thy name,
   Ours is the labour, thine the fame.
   We pray that no harm on thy children may fall,
   That blessing and peace may descend on us all;
   So may we serve thee ever alone,
   Land that we love, our Sierra Leone.

3. Knowledge and truth our forefathers spread,
   Mighty the nations whom they led;
   Mighty they made thee, so too may we
   Show forth the good that is ever in thee.
   We pledge our devotion, our strength and our might,
   Thy cause to defend and to stand for thy right;
   All that we have be ever thine own,
   Land that we love, our Sierra Leone.

SINGAPORE
Majulah Singapura
(May Singapore Progress)

Words and music by
ZUBIR SAID (1907 - 1987)
Arr. by HENRY COLEMAN

For Royal Salute, play from * to *.

First performed in September, 1958. It became very popular and when the country became self-governing on 3 June, 1959, it was decided to make it the National Anthem. It was officially adopted by the Legislative Assembly on 30 November, 1959.

Translation

Let us, the people of Singapore, together march forward towards happiness.
Our noble aspiration is to see Singapore achieve success.
Let us unite in a new spirit.
We all pray: 'May Singapore Progress', 'May Singapore Progress'.

SLOVAKIA

Words by
JANKO MATÚŠKA (1821 - 1877)

Composer unknown *

Allegro energico (♩ = 84)

1. Nad Ta - trou sa blý - ska, hro - my di - vo bi - jú,

nad Ta - trou sa blý - ska, hro - my di - vo bi - jú.

Za - stav - me sa, bra - tia, ved' sa o - ny stra - tia,

* The melody is a Slovak folksong commemorating the exodus of Slovak students from Bratislava in 1843.
On separating from Czechoslovakia on 1 January, 1993, Slovakia retained her section of the former National Anthem as her National Anthem.

2. To Slovensko naše posial' tvrdo spalo,
   To Slovensko naše posial' tvrdo spalo.
   Ale blesky hromu zbudzujú ho k tomu, aby sa prebralo.
   Ale blesky hromu zbudzujú ho k tomu, aby sa prebralo.

Translation

1. Lightning flashes over the Tatra, the thunder pounds wildly,
   Lightning flashes over the Tatra, the thunder pounds wildly,
   Let us pause, brothers, they will surely disappear, the Slovaks will revive,
   Let us pause, brothers, they will surely disappear, the Slovaks will revive.

2. This Slovakia of ours has been fast asleep until now,
   This Slovakia of ours has been fast asleep until now.
   But the thunder and lightning are encouraging it to come alive,
   But the thunder and lightning are encouraging it to come alive.

SLOVENIA

Words by
FRANCE PREŠERN (1800 - 1849)

Music by
STANKO PREMRL (1880 - 1965)
Arr. by W. L. REED

Gaily, energetically

1. Pri - ja - tli o-bro-di - le so tr - te vin-ce nam sla - dko, Ki

nam o - živ - lja ži - le, sr - ce ra-zja-sni in o -

ko, Ki vto-pi vse skr-bi, v po-tr-tih pr-sih up bu - di,

Adopted officially on 27 September, 1989. Slovenia achieved independence on 15 January, 1992.

2. Ži-ve vsi narodi, ki hrepene dočakat dan:
   Da, koder sonce hodi, prepir iz sveta bo pregnan,
   Ko rojak prost bo vsak, ne vrag, le sosed bo mejak,
   Ko rojak prost bo vsak, ne vrag, le sosed bo,
   Ne vrag, le sosed bo mejak.

Translation

1. My friends, the vines have produced again
   Sweet wine which enlivens our veins,
   Clears the eye and the heart,
   Which melts away all our troubles,
   Awakens hope in our sad breast.

2. Long live all nations which long to see the day
   When, wherever the sun shines,
   Strife will be banished from the world!
   All people will be like simple brothers,
   And frontiers will be not enemies, but neighbours!

SOLOMON ISLANDS

Words by
PANAPASA BALEKANA (*b.* 1929)

Music by
PANAPASA BALEKANA (*b.* 1929)
Arr. by W. L. REED

God save our Sol- o- mon Is - lands from shore to shore.

Bless all our peo - ple and all our lands With Your

pro - tect - ing hands. Joy, Peace, Pro - gress and Pro- spe - ri -

Chosen as a result of a competition, and first sung on Independence Day, 7 July, 1978.

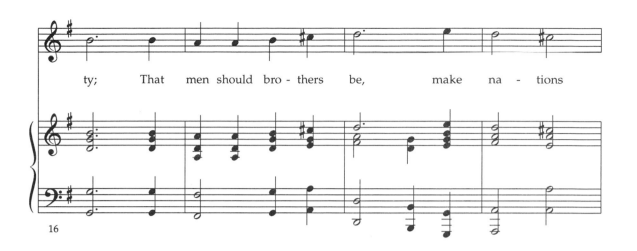

ty; That men should bro - thers be, make na - tions

16

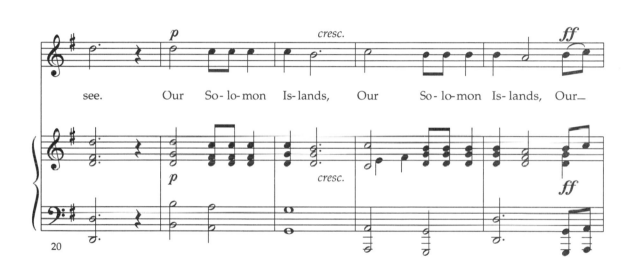

see. Our So- lo-mon Is-lands, Our So- lo-mon Is-lands, Our_

20

na - tion, So- lo-mon Is - lands, Stands for e - ver-more.

25

SOMALIA

No words

Music by
GIUSEPPE BLANC (1886 - 1969)
Arr. by W. L. REED

Adopted in 1960. The National Anthem may have been replaced, but details are as yet unobtainable.

SOUTH AFRICA

Words by
ENOCH MANKAYI SONTONGA (1860 - 1904) and
CORNELIS JACOB LANGENHOVEN (1873 - 1932)

Music by
ENOCH MANKAYI SONTONGA (1860 - 1904) and
MARTHINUS LOURENS DE VILLIERS (1885 - 1977)

With effect from 27 April 1994 South Africa adopted two official National Anthems, 'The Call of South Africa' and 'Nkosi Sikelel' iAfrika'. In May 1995, with Cabinet approval, the National Anthems were shortened and merged into one version for ceremonial purposes. The new version begins with the Nguni and Sotho versions of 'Nkosi Sikelel' iAfrika', continues with the opening lines of 'Die Stem van Suid-Afrika' and ends with an excerpt from the English verison of 'The Call of South Africa'.

he - mel, Uit die diep - te - van ons see, Oor ons e - wi - ge ge -

berg - tes waar die kran - se___ ant - woord gee. Sounds the

call to come to - ge - ther, and u - ni - ted we shall stand, Let us

live and strive for free - dom in South Af - ri - ca, our land.

Translation

(Xhosa and Zulu)
God bless Africa,
Lift her horn on high,
Hear our prayers.
God bless us
Who are Your people.

(Sotho)
God save our nation,
End wars and strife.
South Africa.

(Afrikaans)
Ringing out from our blue heavens, from our deep seas breaking round;
Over everlasting mountains where the echoing crags resound.

SPAIN
Marcha Real
(Royal March)

No words*

Composer unknown
Arr. by W. L. REED

Marziale marcato e sostenuto

The *Marcha Real* dates from 3 September, 1770, when it was declared by Royal Decree of Carlos III as the Spanish Royal March. In July 1942 General Franco issued a decree declaring it as the National Anthem.
*There are no official words, though two writers, Eduardo Marquina (1879 - 1946) and José María Pemán (1897 - 1981) have written verses at different times.

SRI LANKA

Sinhalese words by
ANANDA SAMARAKONE (1911 - 1962)
Author of Tamil words unknown

Music by
ANANDA SAMARAKONE (1911 - 1962)
Arr. by SURYA SENA

Adopted in 1952. There are two additional verses in which the melody is slightly varied.

Translation

Mother Lanka – we salute Thee!
Plenteous in prosperity, Thou,
Beauteous in grace and love,
Laden with corn and luscious fruit
And fragrant flowers of radiant hue,
Giver of life and all good things,
Our land of joy and victory,
Receive our grateful praise sublime,
Lanka! we worship Thee.

SUDAN

Words by
AHMAD MUHAMMAD SALIH (1896 - 1971)

Music by
AHMAD MURJAN (1905 - 1974)
Arr. by T. M. CARTLEDGE

Nah-nu—Djun-dul - lah Djun-dul-wa-tan.

In——— Da A Da Il Гi-da Lam Na-khun.

Na-ta-had-dal Maut End-al-mi-han.

Officially adopted in 1956.

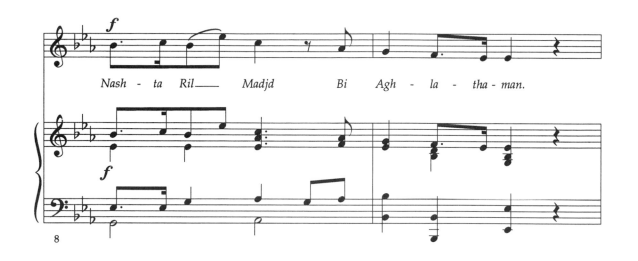

Nash - ta Ril___ Madjd Bi Agh - la - tha - man.

Ha - thi - hil Ard La - na! Fal - ya - ish Su - da - nu - na,

A - la - man Bayn Al U - mam.

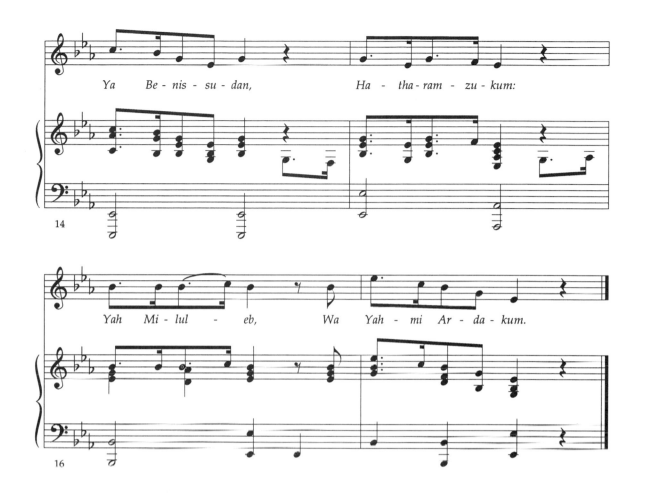

Ya Be - nis - su - dan, Ha - tha - ram - zu - kum:

Yah Mi - lul - eb, Wa Yah - mi Ar - da - kum.

Translation by T. M. Cartledge

We are the army of God and of our land,
We shall never fail when called to sacrifice.
Whether braving death, hardship or pain,
We give our lives as the price of glory.
May this our land, Sudan, live long,
Showing all nations the way.
Sons of the Sudan, summoned now to serve,
Shoulder the task of preserving our country.

SURINAM

Dutch words by
CORNELIS ATSES HOEKSTRA (1852 - 1911)
Sranan version by
HENRY DE ZIEL (1916 - 1975)

Music by
JOHANNES CORSTIANUS DE PUY (1835 - 1924)
Arr. by HENRY COLEMAN

The music was written in 1876, the words in 1893. Officially adopted on 7 December, 1954.

Translation by T. M. Cartledge
(from the Dutch)

God be with our Surinam!
May He glorify our beautiful land!
However we came together here,
We are pledged to your soil.
As we work, let us remember
That justice and truth make us free.
Practising all that is good
Will make our country a worthy land.

SWAZILAND

Words by
ANDREASE ENOKE FANYANA SIMELANE (*b.* 1934)

Music by
DAVID KENNETH RYCROFT (*b.* 1924)

Selected from some 100 entries in a National Anthem competition, when the country attained independence on 6 September, 1968. The composer, Dr. David Rycroft, was formerly Senior Lecturer in Bantu Studies at the School of Oriental and African Studies, University of London, and author of the first siSwati-English dictionary. The National Anthem was composed after ethnomusicological fieldwork in Swaziland and is a compromise between Swazi and Western music. The Swazi musical tradition is unusual in that there are no drums. The stress is on choral dance-songs, with intricate polyphony, rather than on the more usual rhythmic subtleties found elsewhere in Africa.
© Copyright 1969 by David Rycroft.

ni - pha   lo - ku - nge - na - bu - ci -

ni - pha   lo - ku - nge - na - bu - ci -
ni - pha   lo - ku - nge - na - bu - ci -

ka - ni - pha lo - ku - nge - na - bu -

li;   Si - mi - se   u - si - ci - ni -

li;   Si - mi - se   u - si - ci - ni -
li;   Si - mi - se u - si - ci - ni -

(+8va ad lib. _ _ _ _ _ _ _ _ _ _ _ _ _ _ _

ci - li;   Si - mi - se,

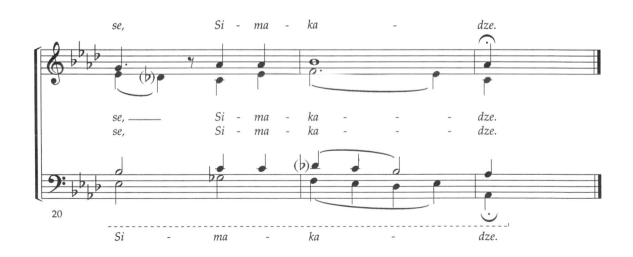

se,   Si - ma - ka - dze.

se, _____ Si - ma - ka - dze.
se,   Si - ma - ka - dze.

Si - ma - ka - dze.

Translation

O Lord our God, bestower of all blessings on the
Swazi;
We give Thee thanks for all our good fortune,
We offer thanks and praise for our King
And for our fair land, its hills and rivers.
Thy blessing be on all rulers of our Country;
Might and power are Thine alone;
We pray Thee to grant us wisdom
Without deceit or malice,
Establish and fortify us,
Lord eternal.

Notes on Pronunciation

Vowels:	There are five vowels: a, e, i, o and u. These are rendered 'pure', much as in Italian, i.e. roughly as 'ah', 'eh', 'ee', 'aw', 'oo'.
Consonants:	Each consonant or consonant cluster belongs with the following vowel, not with the preceding one. Consonant clusters must be treated as single phonemes without being split up, e.g. *neh / tee / ntsah / bah* (Not *neh / teen / tsah-* or *teent / sah-*).

(1)   *ng* has a 'silent g' as in Southern English 'singing' (not as in 'anger').

(2)   *Ng* (in *iNgwenyama* and *Ngwane*) is as in English 'anger'.

(3)   *hl* is a lateral fricative like Welsh double-L, as in 'Llanelly'.

(4)   *dl* is the voiced counterpart of *hl*. (Roughly: French 'j' (as in 'measure') pronounced simultaneously with 'l').

(5)   'c' is a dental click consonant - a purely suction sound produced by withdrawing the tongue-tip from the teeth (with simultaneous velar closure). This sound is sometimes used by English speakers to express annoyance (represented by 'tch' or 'tut-tut'). The following vowel has a 'k'- like onset.

(6)   *ph* is like English 'p'.

(7)   *k* is like English 'g'; *nk* is as in English 'anchor'; kh is like English 'k'.

SWEDEN

Words by
RICHARD DYBECK (1811 - 1877)

Composer unknown
Arr. by EDVIN KALLSTENIUS

Lyrics (sung): 1. Du gam - la, du fri - a, du fjäll - hö - ga Nord, Du tys - ta, du gläd - je - ri - ka skö - - - na! Jag häl - sar dig, vä - nas - te land____ up - på jord, Din

First sung in 1844 with the title 'Sång till Norden' (Song of the North); its use as a National Anthem dates from 1880 - 1890.

sol, din him-mel, di-na äng-der grö - - na, Din

sol din him-mel, di-na äng - der grö - na.

2. *Du tronar på minnen från fornstora da'r,*
   Då ärat ditt namn flög över jorden.
   Jag vet att du är och du blir, vad du var,
   Ja, jag vill leva, jag vill dö i Norden. } (twice)

Translation by T. M. Cartledge

1. You ancient, free and mountainous North,
   Of quiet, joyful beauty,
   I greet you, loveliest land on earth,
   Your sun, your sky, your green meadows. } (twice)

2. You are throned on memories of olden days
   When the honour of your name spread over the earth.
   I know that you are and will remain what you were.
   Oh, may I live, may I die in the Nordic North! } (twice)

SWITZERLAND
Swiss Psalm

Words*
(German) by LEONHARD WIDMER (1808 - 1868)
(French) by CHARLES CHATELANAT (1833 - 1907)
(Italian) by CAMILLO VALSANGIACOMO (1898 - 1978)
(Surselvisch) by ALFONS TUOR (1871 - 1904)
(Ladinisch) by GION ANTONI BÜHLER (1825 - 1897)

Music by
ALBERICH ZWYSSIG (1808 -1854)
Arr. by OTTO KREIS

The original version dates from 1841. Adopted by the Federal Government as the official National Anthem in 1961.
This officially approved arrangement published by Krompholz and Co., Berne.
*The author of the English version is unknown.

Wenn der Al - pen Firn____ sich rö - tet,
Les beau - tés de la____ pa - tri - e
Nel tri - pu - dio del____ mat - ti - no
Cu las bri - schan dall'____ au - ro - ra,
Cur ils munts stra - glu - schan su - ra,

Be - tet, frei - e Schwei - zer, be - tet!
Par - lent à l'âme at - ten - dri - e;
A Te gra - to io____ m'in - chi - no:
U - ra, li - ber Svi - zzer, u - ra!
U - ra, li - ber Svi - zzer, u - ra!

Eu - re from - me See - le ahnt, Eu - re from - me See - le ahnt
Au ciel mon - tent plus joy - eux, Au ciel mon - tent plus joy - eux,
Li - ber - tà, con - cor - dia, a - mor, Li - ber - tà, con - cor - dia, a - mor
Ti has lu in sen - ti - ment, Ti has lu in sen - ti - ment
Ti a or - ma sain - ta ferm, Ti a or - ma sain - ta ferm,

GERMAN

2. Kommst im Abendglüh'n daher,
   Find'ich dich im Sternenheer,
   Dich, du Menschenfreundicher, Liebender!
   In des Himmels lichten Räumen
   Kann ich froh und selig träumen!
   Denn die fromme Seele ahnt   } (twice)
   Gott im hehren Vaterland!
   Gott, im hehren, teuren Vaterland!

3. Ziehst im Nebelflor daher,
   Such' ich dich im Wolkenmeer,
   Dich, du Unergründlicher, Ewiger!
   Aus dem grauen Luftgebilde
   Tritt die Sonne klar und milde,
   Und die fromme Seele ahnt   } (twice)
   Gott im hehren Vaterland!
   Gott, im hehren, teuren Vaterland!

4. Fährst im wilden Sturm daher,
   Bist du selbst uns Hort und Wehr,
   Du, allmächtig Waltender, Rettender!
   In Gewitternacht und Grauen
   Lasst uns kindlich ihm vertrauen!
   Ja, die fromme Seele ahnt   } (twice)
   Gott im hehren Vaterland!
   Gott, im hehren, teuren Vaterland!

2. Lorsqu'un doux rayon du soir
Joue encore dans le bois noir,
Le cœur se sent plus heureux près de Dieu.
Loin des vains bruits de la plaine
L'âme en paix est plus sereine;
Au ciel montent plus joyeux   } (twice)
Les accents d'un cœur pieux,
Les accents émus d'un cœur pieux.

3. Lorsque dans la sombre nuit
La foudre éclate avec bruit,
Notre cœur pressent encore le Dieu fort.
Dans l'orage et la détresse,
Il est notre forteresse.
Offrons-Lui des cœurs pieux,   } (twice)
Dieu nous bénira des cieux,
Dieu nous bénira du haut des cieux.

4. Des grands monts vient le secours,
Suisse! espère en Dieu toujours!
Garde la foi des aïeux, vis comme eux!
Sur l'autel de la partrie
Mets tes biens, ton cœur, ta vie!
C'est le trésor précieux   } (twice)
Que Dieu bénira des cieux,
Que Dieu bénira du haut des cieux.

2. Se di stelle è un giubilo
La celeste sfera,
Te ritrovo a sera,
Ô Signor!
Nella notte silenziosa
L'alma mia in Te riposa:
Libertà, concordia, amor,   } (twice)
All' Elvezia serba ognor!
All' Elvezia serba ognor!

3. Quando tristi velano
Atre nubi il cielo,
Te presente anelo,
Ô Signor!
Se m'ascondi la Tua luce,
Il mio spirito a Te m'adduce:
Libertà, concordia, amor,   } (twice)
All' Elvezia serba ognor!
All' Elvezia serba ognor!

4. Quando rugge e strepita
Impetuoso il nembo,
M'è ostel Tuo grembo,
Ô Signor!
In Te fido, Onnipossente;
Deh, proteggi nostra gente:
Libertà, concordia, amor,   } (twice)
All' Elvezia serba ognor,
All' Elvezia serba ognor!

SURSELVISCH*

2. Cu il serendent sulegl
Resplendescha da smarvegl,
Anflel Tei, miu Creatur,
Amatur!
Vesel nundumbreivlas steilas,
Tarlischontas sco candeilas.
Jeu hai lu in sentiment   } (twice)
De miu Bab sul firmament,
De miu Bab, miu Bab sul firmament.

3. Cu orcans sut il sulegl
Mettan tut en discavegl,
Stai cun mei, o Directur,
Salvatur!
Els orcans ils pli sgarscheivels,
Su cun Tiu agid statteivels,
Jeu hai lu in sentiment   } (twice)
De miu Bab sul firmament,
De miu Bab, miu Bab sul firmament.

*Rhaeto-Romansh of the Rhine valleys.

LADINISCH*

2. *Eir la saira in splendur*
   Da las stailas in l'azur
   Tai chattain nus, creatur,
   Tuotpussant!
   Cur cha 'l firmamaint sclarescha
   In noss cours fidanza crescha.
   Tia orma sainta ferm, } (twice)
   Dieu in tschêl, il Bap etern!
   Dieu in tschêl, il Bap, il Bap etern!

3. *Tü a nus nun est zoppà*
   Cur il tschêl in nüvlas sta,
   Tü imperscrutabel spiert,
   Tuotpussant!
   Tschêl e terra t'obedeschan,
   Vents e nüvlas secundeschan.
   Tia orma sainta ferm, } (twice)
   Dieu in tschêl, il Bap etern!
   Dieu in tschêl, il Bap, il Bap etern!

4. *Eir l'orcan plü furius*
   Nun at muossa main a nus,
   Sco il dirigent dal muond,
   Tuotpussant!
   Eir in temporals terribels
   Sun teis uordens bain visibels.
   Tia orma sainta ferm, } (twice)
   Dieu in tschêl, il Bap etern!
   Dieu in tschêl, il Bap, il Bap etern!

*Rhaeto-Romansh of Engadine.

ENGLISH

1. When the morning skies grow red
   And o'er us their radiance shed,
   Thou, O Lord, appeareth in their light.
   When the Alps glow bright with splendour,
   Pray to God, to Him surrender,
   For you feel and understand, } (twice)
   That He dwelleth in this land. } (twice)

2. In the sunset Thou art nigh
   And beyond the starry sky,
   Thou, O loving Father, ever near.
   When to Heaven we are departing,
   Joy and bliss Thou'lt be imparting,
   For we feel and understand } (twice)
   That Thou dwellest in this land. } (twice)

3. When dark clouds enshroud the hills
   And grey mist the valley fills,
   Yet Thou art not hidden from Thy sons.
   Pierce the gloom in which we cower
   With Thy sunshine's cleansing power;
   Then we'll feel and understand } (twice)
   That God dwelleth in this land. } (twice)

SYRIA

Words by
KHALIL MARDAM BEY (1895 - 1959)

Music by
MOHAMMAD SALIM FLAYFEL (1899 - 1986)
and AHMAD SALIM FLAYFEL (1906 - 1991)

Officially adopted in 1936.

Sa - ma - un La'am - ri - ka Aw Kal - sa - ma.

Translation

Defenders of the realm,
Peace on you;
Our proud spirits will
Not be subdued.
The abode of Arabism,
A hallowed sanctuary;
The seat of the stars,
An inviolable preserve.

Syria's plains are
Towers in the heights,
Resembling the sky
Above the clouds.
A land resplendent
With brilliant suns,
Becoming another sky,
Or almost a sky.

TAIWAN

Words based on a speech by
SUN YAT-SEN (1866 - 1925)

Music by
CHENG MAO-YUN (1900 - 1957)
Arr. by HUANG CHIH and W. L. REED

San min chu I, * wo tang so chung, I kien min kuo, I chin - ta tung. Tze erh to shih, wei min chien feng, su yeh fei shieh, chu I shih tsung, shih

Adopted in 1949.
* The words 'San Min Chu I' express Sun Yat-Sen's political philosophy of the Three People's Principles,
i.e. Government of the people, by the people, and for the people.

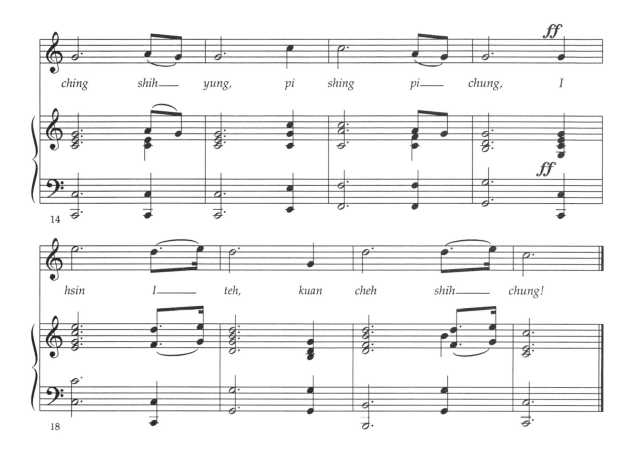

Translation by Tu T'ing-Hsiu

'San min chu I,' our aim shall be,
To found a free land, world peace be our stand.
Lead on comrades, vanguards ye are,
Hold fast your aim, by sun and star,
Be earnest and brave, your country to save,
One heart, one soul, one mind, one goal!

TAJIKISTAN

Music by
SULEIMAN YUDAKOV (*b.* 1916)
Arr. by W. L. REED

Words not yet available.

TANZANIA

Words written collectively

Music by
ENOCH MANKAYI SONTONGA (1860 - 1904)*
Arr. by V. E. WEBSTER

1. Mun - gu i - ba - ri - ki A - fri - ka Wa - ba - ri - ki Vion - go - zi wa - ke He - ki - ma U - mo - ja na A - ma - ni Hi - zi ni ngao— ze - tu A - fri - ka na wa - tu wa - ke.

Adopted when Tanganyika achieved independence on 9 December, 1961 and retained when Tanzania was formed by the union of Tanganyika and Zanzibar on 26 April, 1964. The music is a shorter version of Nkosi Sikelel' iAfrika (see the National Anthems of South Africa and Zambia).

* By permission of Lovedale Press, Cape Province, South Africa.

CHORUS

I - ba - ri - ki A - fri - ka I - ba - ri - ki A - fri - ka

Tu - ba - ri - ki wa - to - to wa A - fri - ka.

2. *Mungu ibariki Tanzania*
Dumisha uhuru na Umoja
Wake kwa Waume na Watoto
Mungu Ibariki
Tanzania na watu wake.

CHORUS
Ibariki Tanzania
Ibariki Tanzania
Tubariki watoto wa Tanzania.

Translation

1. God Bless Africa.
   Bless its leaders.
   Let Wisdom, Unity and Peace
   Be the shield of Africa and its people.

   CHORUS
   Bless Africa,
   Bless Africa,
   Bless the children of Africa.

2. God Bless Tanzania.
   Grant eternal Freedom and Unity
   To its sons and daughters.
   God Bless Tanzania and its people.

   CHORUS
   Bless Tanzania,
   Bless Tanzania,
   Bless the children of Tanzania.

THAILAND

Words by
LUANG SARANUPRAPAN (1896 - 1954)

Music by
PHRA CHEN-DURIYANG (1883 - 1968)

Adopted on 10 December, 1939. Thailand also has a Royal Anthem, with words by HRH Prince Narisasa Nuvativongs (1863-1947) and music by Pyotr Schurovsky (1850-1908) (see NATIONAL ANTHEMS OF THE WORLD – 5th EDITION).

Translation

Thailand embraces in its bosom all people of Thai blood.
Every inch of Thailand belongs to the Thais.
It has long maintained its sovereignty,
Because the Thais have always been united.
The Thai people are peace-loving,
But they are no cowards at war.
They shall allow no one to rob them of their independence,
Nor shall they suffer tyranny.
All Thais are ready to give up every drop of blood
For the nation's safety, freedom and progress.

TOGO

Words and music by
ALEX CASIMIR-DOSSEH (*b.* 1923)
Arr. by ? HASSELMANN* and W. L. REED

1. Sa - lut à toi, pa - ys de nos___ a - ïeux! Toi qui les ren - dais

forts, pai - si - bles et joy - eux, Cul - ti - vant ver - tu, vail - lan - ce___

___ Pour la pos - té - ri - té. Que vien - nent les ty - rans, ton cœur sou - pi - re

Chosen as a result of a competition between Togolese composers. Originally adopted in 1960, it was replaced in 1979, restored in April, 1991 and reconfirmed by the Constitution on 14 October, 1992.
* First name unknown.

vers la li - ber - té. To - go, de - bout! Lut -
tons sans dé - fail - lan - ce, Vain - quons ou mou - rons, mais dans la di - gni - té. Grand Dieu,
Toi seul nous as ex - al - tés Du To - go pour la pros -
pé - ri - té, To - go - lais, viens! Ba - tis - sons la Ci - té!

2. *Dans l'unité nous voulons te servir,*
   C'est bien là de nos cœurs le plus ardent désir.
   Clamons fort notre devise
   Que rien ne peut ternir.
   Seuls artisans de ton bonheur ainsi que de ton avenir,
   Brisons partout les chaînes, la traîtrise
   Et nous te jurons toujours fidélité
   Et aimer, servir, se dépasser,
   Faire encore de toi sans nous lasser
   Togo Chéri, l'Or de l'Humanité.

Translation

1. Hail to thee, land of our forefathers,
   Thou who made them strong, peaceful and happy,
   Men who for posterity cultivated virtue and bravery.
   Even if tyrants shall come, thy heart yearns towards freedom.
   Togo arise! Let us struggle without faltering.
   Victory or death, but with dignity.
   God almighty, Thou alone hast made Togo prosper.
   People of Togo arise! Let us build the nation.

2. To serve thee in unity is the most burning desire of our hearts.
   Let us shout aloud our motto
   That nothing can tarnish.
   We the only builders of thy happiness and of thy future,
   Everywhere let us break chains and treachery,
   And we swear to thee for ever faith, love, service, untiring zeal,
   To make thee yet, beloved Togo, a golden example for humanity.

TONGA

Words by
PRINCE UELINGATONI NGU TUPOUMALOHI (1854 - 1885)

Music by
KARL GUSTAVUS SCHMITT (1834 - 1900)
Arr. by W. L. REED

With devotion (♩ = 66)

'E   'O - tu - a   Ma - fi - ma - fi,   Ko   ho   mau   'Ei -
Oh,   Al - might - y   God   a - bove,   Thou   art   our   Lord   and

ki   Ko   e,   Ko   Koe Koe   fu   la   la   'a - nga,
sure   de - fence,   In   our   good - ness   we   do   trust   Thee

Mo   ia   'o - fa   ki   To - nga;   'A - fio hi - fo
And   our   To - nga   Thou dost   love;   Hear   our prayer,   for

The first reported singing of this National Anthem dates from 1874, but it was probably in use earlier.

'e - mau lo - tu, 'A ia 'o - ku mau fai ni,
though un - seen We know that Thou hast blessed our land;

Mo Ke ta - li ho - mau lo - to, 'O ma - la - 'i 'a Tu - pou.
Grant our earn - est sup - pli - ca - tion, Guard and save Tu - pou our King.

TRINIDAD AND TOBAGO

Words and music by
PATRICK STANISLAUS CASTAGNE (*b.* 1916)

Officially came into use at midnight on 31 August, 1962 at the Flag Raising Ceremony held outside Parliament Buildings, Port of Spain. It was chosen as the result of a competition held by the Government.

TUNISIA

Words by
MUSTAFA SADIK AL-RAFII (1880 - 1937)
and ABOUL KACEM CHABBI (1909 - 1934)

Music by
MOHAMAD ABDEL WAHAB (1915 - 1991)*
Arr. by W. L. REED

Adopted in 1987.
* Mohamad Abdel Wahab also composed the music of the National Anthem of the United Arab Emirates.

Translation by M. A. S. Abdul Haleem

1. *Humāta 'L-himā Yā Humāta 'L-himā*
   Halummū, Halummū, Li-majdi 'Z-zaman
   Laqad Şarakhat Fil-'uruqi 'D-dima
   Namūtu, Namūtu, Wa-yahya 'L-watan
   Li-tadwi 'S-samāwātu Bira'dihā
   Li-tarmi 'Ş-şawā'iqu Nīranahā
   Ilā 'Izzi Tūnis Ilā Majdihā
   Rijāla 'L-bilādi Wa-shubbānahā
   Falā 'Asha Fī Tūnisa Man Khānahā
   Wa-lā 'Asha Man Laysa Min Jundihā
   Namūtu Wa-nahya 'Alā 'Ahdihā
   Hayata 'L-kirami Wa-mawta 'L-'izām.

O defenders of the Homeland!
Rally around to the glory of our time!
The blood surges in our veins,
We die for the sake of our land.
Let the heavens roar with thunder.
Let thunderbolts rain with fire.
Men and youth of Tunisia,
Rise up for her might and glory.
No place for traitors in Tunisia,
Only for those who defend her!
We live and die loyal to Tunisia,
A life of dignity and a death of glory.

2. *Bilādi 'Hkumī wa' Mlikī Wa' Ş'adī*
   Falā 'Asha Man Lam Ya'ish Sayyidā.
   Bihurri Damī Wa-bimā Fī Yadī
   Anā Libilādī Wa-sha'bī Fidā.
   Laki 'L-majdu, Tūnusa, Fa'stamjidī
   Bi'izzati sha'biki Tūla 'L-madā,
   Wa-nahnu usūdu 'L-waghā Fa'shhadī
   Wuthūba Usūdiki Yawma 'Ş-şdidam.

Rule Tunisia! Be wealthy and happy!
Only masters deserve to live
For Tunis and her people.
I give life and wealth.
Glory be yours, Tunisia,
Have full glory
With your people's might forever.
In battles we are lions,
Witness the assault of your lions.

   Warithna 'S-sawā'ida Bayna 'L-umam
   Şukhūran, Şukhūran, Kahādhal 'L'binā
   Sawā'ida Yahtazzu Fawqaha 'L-'alam
   Nubāhī Kihī Wa-yubāhī Binā.
   Wa-fīhā Kafā Li-l 'Ulā Wa'-himam
   Wa-fīhā Li-a'da' I Tūnis Niqam
   Wa-fīhā Li-man Sālamūna' S-salām.

As a nation we inherited
Arms like granite towers.
Holding aloft our proud flag flying,
We boast of it, it boasts of us,
Arms that achieve ambitions and glory,
Sure to realise our hopes,
Inflict defeat on foes,
Offer peace to friends.

   Idha 'Sh-sha'bu Yawman Arāda 'L-hayāh
   Falā Budda An Yastajība 'L-qadar
   Wala Budda Li 'Z-zulmi An Yanjalī
   Wala Budda Li 'L-qaydi An Yankasir.

When the people will to live,
Destiny must surely respond.
Oppression shall then vanish.
Fetters are certain to break.

TURKEY
Istıklâl Marsi
(The March of Independence)

Words by
MEHMET AKIF ERSOY (1873 - 1936)

Music by
OSMAN ZEKİ ÜNGÖR (1880 - 1958)
Arr. by T. M. CARTLEDGE

1. Kork - ma sön - mez bu şa-
fak - - lar - du yü - zen al san - cak Sön - me - den
yur - du - mun üs - tün - de tü - ten en son o - cak. O

The words were adopted in 1921. The music was changed in 1932.

2. Çatma kurban olayım cehreni ey nazlı hilâl
Kahraman ırkıma bir gül ne bu şiddet bu celâl
Sana olmaz dökülen kanlarımız sonra helâl
Hakkıdır hakka tapan milletimin istiklâl.

Translation by T. M. Cartledge

1. Fear not and be not dismayed, this crimson flag will never fade.
   It is the last hearth that is burning for my nation,
   And we know for sure that it will never fail.
   It is my nation's star, shining forever,
   It is my nation's star and it is mine.

2. Frown not, fair crescent, for I am ready to die for you.
   Smile now upon my heroic nation, leave this anger,
   Lest the blood shed for thee be unblessed.
   Freedom is my nation's right,
   Freedom for us who worship God and seek what is right.

TURKMENISTAN

Music by
VELI MUKHATOV (*b.* 1916)
Arr. by W. L. REED

Words not yet available.

TUVALU

Words and music by
AFAESE MANOA (*b.* 1942)
Arr. by W. L. REED

1. "Tu - va - lu mo te A - tu - a" Ko te Fa - ka - vae si - li, Ko te a - lu fo - ki te - na, O te ma - nu - ia ka - toa; Lo - to la - si o fai, Tou ma - lo sao - lo -

1. "Tu - va - lu for The Al - migh - ty" Are the words we hold most dear; For as peo - ple or as lead - ers Of Tu - va - lu we all share In the know - ledge that God E - ver rules in heav'n a -

First sung on Independence Day, 1 October, 1978, when it was officially adopted.

2. *Tuku atu tau pulega*
   Ki te pule mai luga,
   Kilo tonu ki ou mua
   Me ko ia e tautai.
   "Pule tasi mo ia"
   Ki te se gata mai,
   Ko tena mana
   Ko tou malosi tena.
   Pati lima kae kalaga
   Ulufonu ki te tupu.
   "Tuvalu ko tu saoloto"
   Ki te se gata mai.

Translation by J. F. Wilson

2. Let us trust our lives henceforward
   To the King to whom we pray,
   With our eyes fixed firmly on Him,
   He is showing us the way.
   "May we reign with Him in glory"
   Be our song for evermore,
   For His almighty power
   Is our strength from shore to shore.
   Shout aloud in jubilation.
   To the King Whom we adore.
   "Tuvalu free and united"
   Be our song for evermore!

UGANDA

Words and music by
GEORGE WILBERFORCE KAKOMA (b. 1923)

With dignity

1. Oh U - gan - da! may God up - hold thee, We lay our fu - ture in thy hand. U - ni - ted, free, For lib - er - ty To - geth - er we'll al - ways stand.

2. Oh Uganda! the land of freedom,
Our love and labour we give,
And with neighbours all
At our country's call
In peace and friendship we'll live.

3. Oh Uganda! the land that feeds us
By sun and fertile soil grown,
For our own dear land
We'll always stand,
The Pearl of Africa's Crown.

Selected through a competition, and came into use when the country became independent on 9 October, 1962.

UKRAINE

Words by
PAUL CHUBYNSKYI (1839 - 1884)

Music by
MIKHAIL VERBYTSKYI (1815 - 1870)
Arr. by HENRY COLEMAN

Shche ne vmer - la U - kra-i - na, Ni sla - va, ni vo - la,

Shche nam brat - tia mo - lo - di - i U - smikh - net' - sia do - la:

Performed as a choral work in 1864 in the Ukraine Theatre in Lvov, it became officially recognised as the National Anthem in 1917.

Du - shu ti - lo my po - lo - zhym Za na - shu svo - bo - du

I po - ka zhem, shcho my, brat - tia, Ko - zać - ko - ho ro - du.

Translation

Ukraine has not died yet,
As freedom cannot die,
Be hopeful, valiant brothers,
Our glory will revive.
Those who enslave us will perish,
As dew within the sun's ray,
The enlightened rule of kin
Will regain our country.
Willing to give our soul
And body for liberty,   } (twice)
O brothers, we are nearing
The path to victory.

UNITED ARAB EMIRATES

No words

Music by
MOHAMAD ABDEL WAHAB (1915 - 1991)*
Arr. by W. L. REED

Officially adopted in 1971.
*Mohamad Abdel Wahab also composed the music of the National Anthem of Tunisia.

UNITED KINGDOM
God Save The Queen

Author unknown*

Composer unknown

Maestoso

1. God save our gra - cious Queen, Long live our no - ble Queen, God save the Queen: Send her vic - to - ri - ous, Hap - py and glo - ri - ous,

*Earliest copy of the words in Gentleman's Magazine, 1745.

The melody is the same as that of the National Anthem of Liechtenstein. The National Anthem of the United Kingdom is also used in Anguilla, Bermuda, British Virgin Islands, Falkland Islands, Montserrat, Pitcairn Islands, St. Helena and Dependencies and Turks & Caicos Islands. The Cayman Islands have their own National Song.

Long to— reign— o - ver us: God— save the Queen.

2. O Lord our God arise,
   Scatter her enemies,
   And make them fall:
   Confound their politics,
   Frustrate their knavish tricks,
   On Thee our hopes we fix:
   God save us all.

3. Thy choicest gifts in store
   On her be pleased to pour;
   Long may she reign:
   May she defend our laws,
   And ever give us cause
   To sing with heart and voice:
   God save the Queen.

UNITED STATES OF AMERICA
The Star-Spangled Banner

Words by
FRANCIS SCOTT KEY (1779 - 1843)

Composer unknown*

Words and music officially designated as the National Anthem by Act of Congress approved by the President, 3 March, 1931. The National Anthem of the United States of America is also used in American Samoa, Guam, Northern Mariana Islands, Puerto Rico and U.S. Virgin Islands. The United States of America also has fifty State Songs.

* The English composer John Stafford Smith (c. 1750-1836) in his fifth collection of glees (1799) published an arrangement of 'To Anacreon in Heaven', the tune to which Francis Scott Key later wrote 'The Star-Spangled Banner'. This has led to his being mistakenly regarded as the composer of the tune, whose actual origin is unknown.

land_____ of the free and the home of the brave?

23

2. On the shore, dimly seen through the mists of the deep,
   Where the foe's haughty host in dread silence reposes,
   What is that which the breeze, o'er the towering steep,
   As it fitfully blows, half conceals, half discloses?
   Now it catches the gleam of the morning's first beam,
   In full glory reflected now shines on the stream;
   'Tis the Star-Spangled Banner, O long may it wave
   O'er the land of the free and the home of the brave!

3. O thus be it ever when free man shall stand
   Between their loved homes and the war's desolation!
   Blest with victory and peace, may the heaven-rescued land
   Praise the Power that hath made and preserved us a nation.
   Then conquer we must, for our cause it is just,
   And this be our motto: 'In God is our trust.'
   And the Star-Spangled Banner in triumph shall wave
   O'er the land of the free and the home of the brave.

URUGUAY

Words by
FRANCISCO ESTEBAN ACUÑA DE FIGUEROA (1791 - 1862)*

Music by
FRANCISCO JOSÉ DEBALI (1791 - 1859)†
Arr. by G. GRASSO

Officially adopted by a government decree of 18 July, 1845. There are eleven verses.
* Francisco de Figueroa also wrote the words for the National Anthem of Paraguay.
† Francisco José Debali also composed the music for the National Anthem of Paraguay.
Reproduced by permission of Recordi Americana S.A.E.C. Buenos Aires.

sa - bre - mos cum - plir,   sa - bre - mos cum-

27

FINE

plir,   sa - bre - mos cum - plir.   FINE

30

Moderato
_p_ VERSE

¡Li - ber - tad,!   ¡li - ber - tad,!   O - rien - ta   les,   Es - te

_p_ legato

34

_p_

grí - to a la Pa - tria sal - vó!   Que a sus bra - vos en fie - ras ba-

_mf_   _p_

37

557

rien - do tam-bién li - ber-tad!

ff

tam - bién li - ber-tad!

ff

tam - bién li - ber-tad!

D. %% al Fine

f

O - rien-

D. %% al Fine

f

560

Translation by T. M. Cartledge

CHORUS
Eastern landsmen, our country or the tomb! } (twice)
Freedom, or with glory to die!
This is the vow that our souls take
And which we know how, courageously, to fulfil, } (twice)
Know how to fulfil,
Know how to fulfil.   } (three times)

VERSE
Freedom, freedom, eastern landsmen,
This cry saved our country,
Inflaming its brave men } (twice)
With enthusiasm in fierce battles.
We merited the glory of this sacred gift.
Let tyrants tremble!

CHORUS
Let tyrants tremble,
Let tyrants tremble!

VERSE
Ah, in the fight we shall clamour for freedom
And, dying, still cry for it.

CHORUS
In the fight we shall clamour for freedom
And, dying, still cry for it,
And, dying, still cry for it,
Still cry for it,
Still cry for it.

Eastern landsmen... (repeat first six lines). (with internal repeats)

UZBEKISTAN

Words by
ABDULLA ARIPOV (b. 1941)

Music by
MUTAL BURHONOV (b. 1916)
Arr. by W. L. REED

1. *Serquyāsh, hur olkam, elga bakht najāt*
   Sen ozing dostlarin yoldāsh, mehribān!
   Yashnagay ta abad ilmu fan, ijād,
   Shukhrating pārlasin tāki bār jahān!

   CHORUS
   Altin bu vādiylar - jān Ozbekistān,
   Ajdādlār mardāna ruhi senga yār!
   Ulugh khalq qudrati josh urgan zamān,
   Ālamni mahliyā aylagan diyār!

2. *Baghri keng ozbekning ochmas iymāni.*
   Erkin, yāsh avlādlar senga zor qanāt!
   Istiqlāl mash'ali, tinchlik pāsbāni,
   Khaqsevar āna yurt, mangu bol ābād!

   CHORUS

Translation

1. Stand tall, my free country, good fortune and salvation to you,
   You yourself a companion to friends, Oh! Loving one!
   Flourish, Oh! Creator of eternal knowledge and science,
   May your fame for ever shine bright!

   CHORUS
   These valleys are golden - my dear Uzbekistan,
   Our forefathers' manly spirits your companion!
   Strength of great people in turbulent times
   Made this land the world's joy!

2. Oh! Generous Uzbek, your faith will not fade,
   Free, young generations are your mighty wings!
   The torch of independence, guardians of peace,
   Oh! Worthy motherland, flourish and prosper eternally!

   CHORUS

VANUATU

Words and music by
FRANÇOIS VINCENT (*b.* 1955)
Arr. by W. L. REED

Allegro moderato

Yu - mi, Yu - mi, Yu - mi i glat blong ta - lem se, Yu - mi, Yu - mi, Yu - mi i man blong Va - nu - a - tu! 1.God i giv - im ples ia long— yu - mi, Yu - mi

Adopted in 1980.

Yumi, Yumi, Yumi i glat blong talem se,
Yumi, Yumi, Yumi i man blong Vanuatu!

2. *Plante fasin blong bifo i stap,*
   Plante fasin blong tedei,
   Be yumi i olsem wan nomo,
   Hemia fasin blong yumi!

   Yumi, Yumi, Yumi i glat blong talem se,
   Yumi, Yumi, Yumi i man blong Vanuatu!

3. *Yumi save plante wok i stap,*
   Long ol aelan blong yumi,
   God i help em yumi evriwan,
   Hemi papa blong yumi.

   Yumi, Yumi, Yumi i glat blong talem se,
   Yumi, Yumi, Yumi i man blong Vanuatu!

Translation by Parai K. Tamei

We are happy to proclaim
We are the People of Vanuatu !

1. God has given us this land;
   This gives us great cause for rejoicing.
   We are strong, we are free in this land;
   We are all brothers.

   We are happy to proclaim
   We are the People of Vanuatu !

2. We have many traditions
   And we are finding new ways.
   Now we shall be one People,
   We shall be united for ever.

   We are happy to proclaim
   We are the People of Vanuatu!

3. We know there is much work to be done
   On all our islands.
   May God, our Father, help us!

   We are happy to proclaim
   We are the People of Vanuatu!

VATICAN CITY STATE
Inno e Marcia Pontificale
(Hymn and Pontifical March)

Words by
ANTONIO ALLEGRA (1905 - 1969)

Music by
CHARLES GOUNOD (1818 - 1893)

This became the official hymn in 1950. It is played (1) In the presence of the Holy Father. (2) In the presence of one of his Special Legates. (3) On the occasion of presentation of Credential Letters by a Nuncio of the Holy See. There are also Latin words, written by Raffaello Lavagna (b. 1918).

568

gno - re,___ Pa - ce_ai___ Fe - de - li, di Cri - sto nel - l'a -

mo - re. A___ Te ve - nia - mo, An - ge - li - co Pa -

sto - re, In___ Te ve dia mo il___ mi te Re - den -

to - re, E - re - de San - to di ve - ra e san - ta

Marcia Pontificale (Pontifical March)

Sal - ve, Sal - ve Ro - ma, pa - tria e - ter - na di me -

mo - rie, Can - ta - no le tue glo - ri - e, mil - le

pal - me e mil - le al - ta - ri. Ro - ma de - gli A-

po - sto - li, Ma - dre e gui - da dei Re - den - ti,

Ro - ma de - gli A-po - sto - li, Ma - dre e gui - da dei Re - den - ti,

Ro - ma lu - ce del - le gen - ti, il mon - do spe - ra in te!_____

Translation

HYMN	PONTIFICAL MARCH

<table>
<tr>
<td>

O Rome immortal, city of martyrs and saints,
O immortal Rome, accept our praises.
Glory in the heavens to God our Lord
And peace to men who love Christ!

To you we come, angelic Pastor,
In you we see the gentle Redeemer.
You are the holy heir of our Faith,
You are the comfort and the refuge of
   those who believe and fight.

Force and terror will not prevail,
But truth and love will reign.

</td>
<td>

Hail, O Rome,
Eternal abode of memories;
A thousand palms and a thousand altars
Sing your praises.

O city of the Apostles,
Mother and guide of the elect,
Light of the nations,
And hope of the world!

Hail, O Rome!
Your light will never fade;
The splendour of your beauty
Disperses hatred and shame.

O city of the Apostles,
Mother and guide of the elect,
Light of the nations,
And hope of the world!

</td>
</tr>
</table>

VENEZUELA

Words by
VICENTE SALIAS (1786 - 1814)

Music by
JUAN JOSÉ LANDAETA (1780 - 1814)

Adopted on 25 May, 1881, by a government decree.

fó;   A es - te san - to nom - bre,   A es - te san - to nom - bre

Tem - bló de pa - vor,   El vil e - go - is - mo Que o - tra vez triun -

rit.

a tempo

fó,   El vil e - go - is - mo   Que o - tra vez triun - fó.

D.C. al Fine

2. *Gritemos con brío:*
   Muera la opresión!
   Compatriotas fieles
   La fuerza es la unión:
   Y desde el Empíreo
   El Supremo Autor,
   Un sublime aliento
   Al pueblo infundió.

   CHORUS

3. *Unida con lazos*
   Que el cielo formó,
   La América toda
   Existe en Nación;
   Y si el despotismo
   Levanta la voz,
   Seguid el ejemplo
   Que Caracas dió.

   CHORUS

Translation by T. M. Cartledge

CHORUS
Glory to the brave nation
Which shook off the yoke,   } (twice)
Respecting law, virtue and honour.

SOLO
"Off with the chains! Off with the chains!"   (repeated phrase by CHORUS)
Cried the Lord, cried the Lord,   (repeated phrase by CHORUS)
And the poor man in his hovel
Implored freedom.
At this holy name, there trembled
The vile selfishness that had triumphed,
The vile selfishness that had triumphed.

CHORUS
Glory to the brave nation... etc. (repeat top 3 lines, with internal repeat)

2. Let's cry out aloud:
   Down with oppression!
   Faithful countrymen, your strength
   Lies in your unity;
   And from the heavens
   The supreme Creator
   Breathed a sublime spirit
   Into the nation.

   CHORUS

3. United by bonds
   Made by heaven,
   All America exists
   As a Nation;
   And if tyranny
   Raises its voice,
   Follow the example
   Given by Caracas.

   CHORUS

VIETNAM

Words and music by
NGUYEN VAN CAO (1923 - 1995)

Adopted by the Provisional Government of the Democratic Republic of Vietnam from the first days of its formation, and by the National Assembly in its second session in November, 1946. In July, 1976 the first election of the United National Assembly adopted this National Anthem for the whole of the country.

1. *Soldats vietnamiens, nous allons de l'avant,*
   Mus par une même volonté de sauver la patrie.
   Nos pas redoublés sonnent sur la route longue et rude.
   Notre drapeau, rouge du sang de la victoire, porte l'âme de la nation.
   Le lointain grondement des canons rythme les accents de notre marche.
   Le chemin de la gloire se pave de cadavres ennemis.
   Triomphant des difficultés, ensemble, nous édifions nos bases de résistance.
   Jurons de lutter sans répit pour la cause du peuple.
   Courons vers le champ de bataille!
   En avant! Tous ensemble, en avant!
   Notre patrie vietnamienne est solide et durable.

2. *Soldats vietamiens, nous allons de l'avant,*
   L'etoile d'or au vent
   Conduisant notre peuple et notre patrie hors de la misère et des souffrances.
   Unissons nos efforts dans la lutte pour l'édification de la vie nouvelle.
   Debout! d'un même élan, rompons nos fers!
   Depuis si longtemps, nous avons contenu notre haine!
   Soyons prêts à tous les sacrifices et notre vie sera radieuse.
   Jurons de lutter sans répit pour la cause du peuple,
   Courons vers le champ de bataille!
   En avant! Tous ensemble, en avant!
   Notre patrie vietnamienne est solide et durable.

Translation

1. Soldiers of Vietnam, we go forward,
   With the one will to save our Fatherland,
   Our hurried steps are sounding on the long and arduous road.
   Our flag, red with the blood of victory, bears the spirit of our country.
   The distant rumbling of the guns mingles with our marching song.
   The path to glory passes over the bodies of our foes.
   Overcoming all hardships, together we build our resistance bases.
   Ceaselessly for the people's cause let us struggle,
   Let us hasten to the battle-field !
   Forward! All together advancing!
   Our Vietnam is strong, eternal.

2. Soldiers of Vietnam, we go forward!
   The gold star of our flag in the wind
   Leading our people, our native land, out of misery and suffering.
   Let us join our efforts in the fight for the building of a new life.
   Let us stand up and break our chains.
   For too long have we swallowed our hatred.
   Let us keep ready for all sacrifices and our life will be radiant.
   Ceaselessly for the people's cause let us struggle,
   Let us hasten to the battle-field!
   Forward! All together advancing!
   Our Vietnam is strong, eternal.

WALES
Hen Wlad fy Nhadau
(Land of my Fathers)

Words by
EVAN JAMES (1809 - 1893)
English versification by
W. S. GWYNN WILLIAMS

Music by
JAMES JAMES (1833 - 1902)
Arr. by W. S. GWYNN WILLIAMS
and W. L. REED

1. Mae hen wlad fy / nhad-au yn an nwyl i mi, Gwlad beirdd a chan-tor-ion, en- / wog-ion o fri; Ei gwr-ol ry-fel-wyr, gwlad-gar-wyr tra-

1. The land of my / fath-ers is dear un-to me, Old land where the min-strels are / hon-oured and free; Its war-ring de-fen-ders so gal-lant and—

First sung at the famous Llangollen Eisteddfod of 1858, and now regarded as having the status of a National Anthem.
It is also sung as an anthem in Brittany, to a Breton version by J. Taldir.
English versification by permission of the Gwyn Publishing Co. (Copyright 1950).

mâd, Tros rydd - id coll - as - ant eu gwaed.
brave, For free - dom their life's blood they gave.

f CHORUS

Gwlad, gwlad, pleid - iol wyf i'm
Home, home, true am I to

gwlad, Tra môr yn fur i'r bur hoff
home, While seas se - cure the land so

D. 𝄋

bau, O bydd - ed i'r hen - iaith bar - hau.
pure, O may the old lan - guage en - dure.

2. *Hen Gymru fynyddig, paradwys y bardd,*
   Pob dyffryn, pob clogwyn i'm golwg sydd hardd;
   Trwy deimlad gwladgarol, mor swynol yw si
   Ei nentydd, afonydd, i mi.

   CHORUS

3. *Os treisiodd y gelyn fy ngwlad tan ei droed,*
   Mae hen iaith y Cymry mor fyw ag erioed;
   Ni Iuddiwyd yr awen gan erchyll law brad,
   Na thelyn berseiniol fy ngwlad.

   CHORUS

2. Old land of the mountains, the Eden of bards,
   Each gorge and each valley a loveliness guards;
   Through love of my country, charmed voices will be
   Its streams, and its rivers, to me.

   CHORUS

3. Though foemen have trampled my land 'neath their feet,
   The language of Cambria still knows no retreat;
   The muse is not vanquished by traitor's fell hand,
   Nor silenced the harp of my land.

   CHORUS

WESTERN SAMOA
The Banner of Freedom

Words and music by
SAUNI IIGA KURESA (1900 - 1978)
Arr. by HENRY COLEMAN

On 1 January, 1962 Western Samoa became the first sovereign independent Polynesian State. Selected by the Council of the Committee to be the National Anthem, it was sung as the flag of the Western Samoan Government was raised.

Translation

Samoa, arise and raise your banner that is your crown!
Oh! see and behold the stars on the waving banner!
They are a sign that Samoa is able to lead.
Oh! Samoa, hold fast
Your freedom for ever!
Do not be afraid; as you are founded on God;
Our treasured precious liberty.
Samoa, arise and wave
Your banner that is your crown!

YEMEN

Words by
ABDULLA ABDUL WAHAB NOMAN (*c.* 1916 - 1982)

Music by
AYOOB TARISH (*b.* 1943)
Arr. by W. L. REED

Adopted on 22 May, 1990. The union of South Yemen (People's Republic) and North Yemen (Arab Republic) took place on 22 May, 1990. The National Anthem of South Yemen was retained.

Raddidī Ayyatuha 'D-dunyā Nashīdī
Raddidīhī Wa-a 'īdī Wa-a 'īdī
Wa 'Dhkurī Fī Farhatī Kulla Shahīdi
Wa'Mnaḥīhī Ḥullalan Min Ḍaw'i 'Īdī
Raddidī Ayyatuha 'D-dunyā Nashīdī
'Ishtu Īmānī Wa-ḥubbī Umamiyyā
Wa-masīrī Fawqa Darbī 'Arabiyyā
Wa-sayabqā Nabḍu Qalbī Yamaniyyā
Lan Tarā 'D-dunyā 'Alā Arḍī Waṣiyyā.

Translation by M. A. S. Abdul Haleem

Repeat, O World, my song.
Echo it over and over again.
Remember, through my joy, each martyr.
Clothe him with the shining mantles
Of our festival.
Repeat, O World, my song.
In faith and love I am part of mankind.
An Arab I am in all my life.
My heart beats in tune with Yemen.
No foreigner shall dominate over Yemen.

YUGOSLAVIA
(SERBIA AND MONTENEGRO)

Words by
SAMUEL TOMAŠIK (1813 - 1887)

Composer unknown
Arr. by BORIVOJE SIMIĆ

Originally composed about the middle of the 19th. century as an anthem of the Slavonic movement for the Union of Slavs.
It became the National Anthem of Yugoslavia in 1945. The melody resembles that of the National Anthem of Poland. A
new National Anthem may be expected, and the country renamed.

Ži - ve - će ve - kov' - ma, Za - lud pre - ti po - nor pa - kla,

Za - lud va - tra gro - ma, Za - lud va - tra gro - ma!

Translation

2. *Nek se sada i nad nama*
   Burom sve raznese,
   Stena puca, dub se lama,
   Zemlja nek se trese.
   Mi stojimo postojano
   Kano klisurine;
   Proklet bio izdajica
   Svoje domovine! } (twice)

1. Hey Slavs! our grandfathers' word still lives,
   As long as their sons' heart beats for the people.
   It lives, the spirit of Slavs lives, it will live for centuries,
   The abyss of hell threatens in vain, the fire of thunder is in vain.

2. Now let everything above us be carried away by the bura.*
   The rock cracks, the oak breaks, let the ground shake.
   We stand steadfastly like cliffs;
   Let the traitor of his homeland be damned!

*A fast and sudden north-east wind, which blows along the eastern Adriatic coast.

ZAÏRE

Words and music by
BOKA DI MPASI LONDI (*b.* 1929)
Arr. by T. M. CARTLEDGE

Za - ï - rois, dans la paix —— re - trou - vée, Peu - ple u -
ni, nous som - mes Za - ï - rois. En a - vant, fier et plein de di - gni -

Adopted in 1972.

al   Qui nous re - lie aux a - ïeux, à nos en - fants: Paix, Jus -

tice et Tra - vail,   Paix, Jus - tice et Tra - vail.

Translation

Zaïrians, in refound peace
We are a united people, Zaïrians.
Forward with pride and dignity,
A great people, for ever free!
O Tricolour, kindle the sacred fire in us
So that we may build our country finer yet,
Beside a 'Kingly River',
Beside a 'Kingly River'.
Waving Tricolour, revive the ideal
Which binds us to our forbears and our children:
Peace, Justice and Work,
Peace, Justice and Work.

ZAMBIA

Words written collectively

Music by
ENOCH MANKAYI SONTONGA (1860 - 1904)*
Arr. by MRS. WALTERS and D. W. DUNN

1. Stand and sing of Zam-bia, proud and free, Land of work and joy in u-ni-ty, Vic-tors in the strug-gle for the right, We've won We have won free-dom's fight. All one,
2. A-fri-ca is our own mo-ther-land, Fash-ion'd with and blessed by God's good hand, Let us all her peo-ple join as one, Bro-thers un-der the sun. All one,
3. One land and one na-tion is our cry, Dig-ni-ty and peace 'neath Zam-bia's sky, Like our no-ble ea-gle in its flight, Zam-bia, praise to thee. All one,

(S.T.)

(T.B.) in the sun.

*Originally written as a hymn tune at Lovedale Mission in Cape Province, South Africa.

The tune became well known throughout a large part of southern, central and eastern Africa, and the words were translated into many African languages. Indeed, it came to be popularly known as the Bantu National Anthem. The tune was officially adopted by Tanganyika (later Tanzania) as its National Anthem on the achievement of independence in 1961. New words have been specially written for Zambia. A competition was held and these words were produced as a composite version after a study of the ideas and the words of the six leading entries in the competition.

Officially adopted 24 October, 1964. It was also adopted as part of the National Anthem of South Africa in 1994.

1. *Lumbanyeni Zambia, no kwanga,*
   Ne cilumba twange tuumfwane,
   Mpalume sha bulwi bwa cine,
   Twaliilubula.
   Twikatane bonse.

2. *Bonse tuli bana ba Africa,*
   Uwasenaminwa na Lesa,
   Nomba bonse lwendele pamo,
   Twaliilubula.
   Twikatane bonse.

3. *Fwe lukuta lwa Zambia lonse,*
   Twikatane tubyo mutende,
   Pamo nga lubambe mu mulu,
   Lumbanyeni Zambia.
   Twikatane bonse.

   CHORUS (after 3rd verse only)
   Lumbanyeni,
   Lesa, Lesa, wesu,
   Apale calo,
   Zambia, Zambia, Zambia.
   Fwe bantungwa
   Mu luunga lwa calo.
   Lumbanyeni Zambia.
   Twikatane bonse.

ZIMBABWE

Kalibusiswe Ilizwe leZimbabwe
Blessed be the Land of Zimbabwe

Words by
SOLOMON MUTSWAIRO (*b.* 1924)

Music by
FRED LECTURE CHANGUNDEGA (*b.* 1954)
Arr. by W. L. RRED

Officially adopted on 18 April, 1994.

(Ndebele)

2. *Khangelan' i Zimbabwe yon' ihlotshi si we*
   Ngezintaba lang' miful' e bu keka yo.
   I zulu kaline, izilimo zande;
   Iz' sebenzi zenam', abantu basuthe;
   Kalibusiswe ilizwe leZimbabwe.

3. *Nkosi bu sis' ilizwe le-thu leZimbabwe*
   Ilizwe labo khokho bethu thina sonke;
   Kusuk' eZambezi Kusiy' e Limpopo.
   Abakho kheli babe lobuqotho;
   Kalibusiswe ilizwe leZimbabwe.

(Shona)

2. *Tarisai Zimbabwe nyika yakashonge dzwa*
   Namakomo, nehova, zvinoyeve dza;
   Mvura ngainaye, minda ipe mbesa
   Vashandi vatuswe, ruzhinji rugutswe;
   Ngaikomborerwe nyika yeZimbabwe.

3. *Mwari ropafadzai nyika yeZimbabwe*
   Nyika yamadzitate guru edu to se;
   Kubva Zambezi Kusvika Limpopo,
   Navatungamiri vave nenduramo;
   Ngaikomborerwe nyika yeZimbabwe.

(English)

2. O lovely Zimbabwe, so wondrously adorned
   With mountains and rivers cascading, flowing free;
   May rain abound, and fertile fields.
   May we be fed, our labour blessed;
   And may the Almighty protect and bless our land.

3. O God, we beseech Thee to bless our native land;
   The land of our fathers bestowed upon us all;
   From Zambezi to Limpopo.
   May leaders be exemplary;
   And may the Almighty protect and bless our land.

EUROPEAN COMMUNITY

Music by
LUDWIG van BEETHOVEN (1770 - 1827)
Arr. by W. L. REED

The Anthem is the Prelude to 'Ode of Joy' from the fourth movement of the Ninth Symphony by Ludwig van Beethoven, chosen as the European Anthem by the Council of Europe in 1971-1972. There are words in German, but they are not sung at European Community events.

NATIONAL DAYS

AFGHANISTAN	27 April	Anniversary of the Saur Revolution, 1978
ALBANIA	11 January	National Day, 1946
ALGERIA	1 November	National Day, 1954
ANDORRA	8 September	Jungfrau von Meritxell Day, 1874
ANGOLA	11 November	Independence Day, 1975
ANTIGUA and BARBUDA	1 November	Independence Day, 1981
ARGENTINA	25 May	National Day, 1810
ARMENIA	23 September	Independence Day, 1991
AUSTRALIA	26 January	Australia Day, 1788
AUSTRIA	26 October	National Day, 1955
AZERBAIJAN	28 May	Independence Day, 1918
BAHAMAS, THE	10 July	Independence Day, 1973
BAHRAIN	16 December	National Day, 1961
BANGLADESH	26 March	Independence Day, 1971
BARBADOS	30 November	Independence Day, 1966
BELARUS	27 July	Independence Day, 1990
BELGIUM	6 June	Birthday of H.M. King Albert II, 1934
	21 July	Independence Day, 1831
BELIZE	21 September	Independence Day, 1981
BÉNIN	30 November	Independence Day, 1975
BHUTAN	11 November	Birthday of H.M. King Jigme Singye Wangchuck, 1955
	17 December	National Day, 1907
BOLIVIA	6 August	Independence Day, 1825
BOSNIA HERZEGOVINA	6 April	Independence Day, 1992
BOTSWANA	30 September	Independence Day, 1966
BRAZIL	7 September	Independence Day 1822
BRUNEI DARUSSALAM	23 February	National Day, 1984
BULGARIA	9 September	National Day, 1944
BURKINA FASO	4 August	National Day, 1984
BURUNDI	1 July	Independence Day, 1962
CAMBODIA	17 April	National Day, 1976
	31 October	Birthday of H.M. King Norodom Sihanouk, 1922
CAMEROON	20 May	National Day, 1972
CANADA	1 July	Canada Day, 1867
CAPE VERDE	5 July	Independence Day, 1975
CENTRAL AFRICAN REPUBLIC	1 December	National Day, 1958
CHAD	11 August	National Day, 1960
CHILE	18 September	Independence Day, 1810
CHINA	1 October	Proclamation of Provisional Constitution, 1949
COLOMBIA	20 July	National Independence Day, 1810
COMOROS, THE	6 July	Independence Day, 1975
CONGO	15 August	Independence Day, 1960
COSTA RICA	15 September	Independence Day, 1821
CROATIA	30 May	Independence Day, 1991
CUBA	1 January	National Day, 1959
CYPRUS	1 October	National Day, 1963
CZECH REPUBLIC	8 May	Liberation Day, 1945
	28 October	Founding of the Republic, 1918

DENMARK	16 April	Birthday of H.M. Queen Margrethe II, 1940
DJIBOUTI	27 June	Independence Day, 1977
DOMINICA	3 November	Independence Day, 1978
DOMINICAN REPUBLIC	27 February	Independence Day, 1844
ECUADOR	10 August	Independence Day, 1809
EGYPT	23 July	National Day, 1952
EL SALVADOR	15 September	Independence Day, 1821
ENGLAND	23 April	Saint George's Day, 1415
EQUATORIAL GUINEA	12 October	Independence Day, 1968
ERITREA	24 May	Independence Day, 1993
ESTONIA	24 February	National Day, 1918
ETHIOPIA	28 May	Victory Day, 1991
FIJI	10 October	Independence Day, 1970
FINLAND	6 December	Independence Day, 1917
FRANCE	14 July	Bastille Day, 1789
GABON	17 August	Independence Day, 1960
GAMBIA, THE	18 February	Independence Day, 1965
GEORGIA	26 May	Independence Day, 1991
GERMANY	23 May	Constitution Day, 1949
GHANA	6 March	Independence Day, 1957
GIBRALTAR	10 September	National Day, 1993
GREECE	25 March	Independence Day, 1821
GRENADA	7 February	Independence Day, 1974
GUATEMALA	15 September	Independence Day, 1821
GUINEA	2 October	Independence Day, 1958
GUINEA - BISSAU	24 September	National Day, 1974
GUYANA	23 February	Republic Day, 1970
	26 May	Independence Day, 1966
HAITI	1 January	Independence Day, 1804
HONDURAS	15 September	Independence Day, 1821
HUNGARY	15 March	National Day, 1991
	20 August	Saint Stephen's Day, 1990
	23 October	Anniversary of the Revolution, 1956 and Proclamation of the Hungarian Republic, 1989
ICELAND	17 June	Anniversary of Establishment of the Republic, 1944
INDIA	26 January	Republic Day, 1950
INDONESIA	17 August	Independence Day, 1945
IRAN	11 February	National Day, 1978
IRAQ	17 July	National Day, 1968
IRISH REPUBLIC	17 March	Saint Patrick's Day, 1681
ISLE OF MAN	5 July	National Day, 1752
ISRAEL	15 May	Independence Day, 1948
ITALY	2 June	Anniversary of Proclamation of the Republic, 1946
IVORY COAST	7 December	Independence Day, 1960

JAMAICA	6 August	Independence Day, 1962
	(This is celebrated the First Monday of August each year)	
JAPAN	23 December	Birthday of H.M. Emperor Akihito, 1933
JORDAN	25 May	Independence Day, 1946
	14 November	Birthday of H.M. King Hussein, 1935
KAZAKHSTAN	16 December	Independence Day, 1991
KENYA	12 December	Independence Day, 1963 and Republic Day, 1964
KIRIBATI	12 July	Independence Day, 1979
KOREA (North)	8 September	Constitution Day, 1948
KOREA (South)	15 August	Independence Day, 1948
KUWAIT	25 February	National Day, 1961
KYRGYZSTAN	31 August	Independence Day, 1991
LAOS	2 December	National Day, 1975
LATVIA	18 November	National Day, 1918
LEBANON	22 November	Independence Day, 1943
LESOTHO	17 July	Birthday of H.M. King Letsie III, 1963
	4 October	Independence Day, 1966
LIBERIA	26 July	Independence Day, 1847
LIBYA	1 September	National Day, 1969
LIECHTENSTEIN	14 February	Birthday of H.S.H. Prince Hans Adam II, 1945
	15 August	National Day, 1940
LITHUANIA	16 February	Independence Day, 1918
LUXEMBOURG	5 January	Birthday of H.R.H. Grand Duke Jean, 1921
	23 June	National Day, 1962
MACEDONIA	8 September	Independence Day, 1991
MADAGASCAR	26 June	Proclamation of Independence of the Republic, 1960
MALAWI	6 July	Independence Day, 1964 and Republic Day, 1966
MALAYSIA	31 August	National Day, 1957
MALDIVES, THE	26 July	Independence Day, 1965
MALI	22 September	Independence Day, 1960
MALTA	21 September	Independence Day, 1964
MARSHALL ISLANDS	21 October	Compact Day, 1986
MAURITANIA	28 November	Independence Day, 1960
MAURITIUS	12 March	Independence Day, 1968
MEXICO	16 September	National Day, 1810
MICRONESIA	10 May	Constitution Day, 1979
	3 November	Compact Day, 1986
MOLDOVA	27 August	Independence Day, 1991
MONACO	31 May	Birthday of H.S.H. Prince Rainier III, 1923
	19 November	Saint Rainier Day, 1949
MONGOLIA	11 July	National Day, 1921
MOROCCO	3 March	Anniversary of the Throne, 1956
	9 July	Birthday of H.M. King Hassan II, 1929
MOZAMBIQUE	25 June	Independence Day, 1975
MYANMAR	4 January	Independence Day, 1948
NAMIBIA	21 March	Independence Day, 1990
NAURU	31 January	National Day, 1968

NEPAL	18 February	National Democracy Day, 1952
	28 December	Birthday of H.M. King Birendra, 1945
NETHERLANDS	31 January	Birthday of H.M. Queen Beatrix, 1938
	5 May	Liberation Day, 1945
NEW ZEALAND	6 February	Waitangi Day, 1840
NICARAGUA	15 September	Independence Day, 1821
NIGER	18 December	National Day, 1958
NIGERIA	1 October	Republic Day, 1960
NORWAY	21 February	Birthday of H.M. King Harald V, 1937
	17 May	Constitution Day, 1814
OMAN	18 November	National Day, 1971
PAKISTAN	23 March	Republic Day, 1956
	14 August	Independence Day, 1947
PALAU	9 July	Constitution Day, 1979
	1 October	Independence Day, 1994
PANAMA	3 November	Independence Day, 1903
PAPUA NEW GUINEA	16 September	Independence Day, 1975
PARAGUAY	15 May	Independence Day, 1811
PERU	28 July	Independence Day, 1821
PHILIPPINES, THE	12 June	Independence Day, 1898
POLAND	3 May	Constitution Day, 1989
PORTUGAL	10 June	National Day, 1880
QATAR	3 September	Independence Day, 1971
ROMANIA	23 August	Liberation Day, 1944
RUSSIAN FEDERATION	26 December	National Day, 1991
RWANDA	1 July	Independence Day, 1962
SAINT KITTS and NEVIS	19 September	Independence Day, 1983
SAINT LUCIA	22 February	Independence Day, 1979
SAINT VINCENT and THE GRENADINES	27 October	Independence Day, 1979
SAN MARINO	3 September	National Day, 301
SÃO TOMÉ and PRÍNCIPE	12 July	Independence Day, 1975
SAUDI ARABIA	20 May	Independence Day, 1927
	23 September	National Day, 1964
SCOTLAND	30 November	Saint Andrew's Day, 832
SÉNÉGAL	4 April	Independence Day, 1960
SEYCHELLES	18 June	National Day, 1977
SIERRA LEONE	27 April	Independence Day, 1961
SINGAPORE	9 August	Independence Day, 1965
SLOVAKIA	1 January	Independence Day, 1993
SLOVENIA	25 June	Independence Day, 1991
SOLOMON ISLANDS	7 July	Independence Day, 1978
SOMALIA	21 October	National Day, 1969
SOUTH AFRICA	31 May	Republic Day, 1961
SPAIN	5 January	Birthday of H.M. King Juan Carlos, 1938
	12 October	National Day, 1918
SRI LANKA	4 February	Independence Commemoration Day, 1948

SUDAN	1 January	Independence Day, 1956
SURINAM	25 November	Independence Day, 1975
SWAZILAND	19 April	Birthday of H.M. King Mswati III, 1968
	6 September	Independence Day, 1968
SWEDEN	30 April	Birthday of H.M. King Carl XVI Gustaf, 1946
	6 June	National Day, 1983
SWITZERLAND	1 August	Anniversary of the Foundation of Confederation, 1291
SYRIA	17 April	National Day, 1943
TAIWAN	10 October	National Day, 1911
TAJIKISTAN	9 September	Independence Day, 1991
TANZANIA	26 April	Tanzanian Union Day, 1964
THAILAND	6 April	Chakri Day, 1782
	23 October	Chulalongkorn Day, 1910
	5 December	Birthday of H.M. King Bhumibol Adulyadej, 1927
TOGO	13 January	National Liberation Day, 1963
TONGA	4 June	Independence Day, 1970
	4 July	Birthday of H.M. King Tupou IV, 1918
TRINIDAD and TOBAGO	31 August	Independence Day, 1962
	24 September	Republic Day, 1976
TUNISIA	20 March	Independence Day, 1956
TURKEY	29 October	Proclamation of the Republic, 1923
TURKMENISTAN	27 October	Independence Day, 1991
TUVALU	1 October	Independence Day, 1978
UGANDA	9 October	Independence Day, 1962
UKRAINE	24 August	Independence Day, 1991
UNITED ARAB EMIRATES	2 December	Independence Day, 1971
UNITED KINGDOM	21 April	Birthday of H.M. Queen Elizabeth II, 1926
UNITED STATES OF AMERICA	4 July	Independence Day, 1776
	27 November	Thanksgiving Day, 1621
	(This is celebrated the Fourth Thursday of November each year)	
URUGUAY	25 August	Independence Day, 1825
UZBEKISTAN	31 August	Independence Day, 1991
VANUATU	30 July	Independence Day, 1980
VATICAN CITY STATE	18 May	Birthday of H.H. Pope John Paul II, 1920
	22 October	National Day, 1978
VENEZUELA	5 July	Independence Day, 1811
VIETNAM	2 September	National Day, 1945
WALES	1 March	Saint David's Day, 1398
WESTERN SAMOA	1 June	National Day, 1962
YEMEN	22 May	National Unity Day, 1990
YUGOSLAVIA	29 November	National Day, 1945
ZAÏRE	24 November	National Day, 1965
ZAMBIA	24 October	Independence Day, 1964
ZIMBABWE	18 April	Independence Day, 1980
EUROPEAN COMMUNITY	9 May	Europe Day, 1985
UNITED NATIONS	24 October	United Nations Day, 1945